Think Slim-Be Slim

About the Author

Elsye Birkinshaw is the director and founder of the Seminars of Self-Awareness Center, conducting highly successful classes in the western states–including regular programs for California State University Extension–soon to be expanded throughout the United States. These classes have proven to be effective in behavior modification in relation to problems of compulsive eating, smoking, inferiority feelings, emotional problems, and the problems of aging.

Think Slim-
Be Slim

A new 21-day plan for "mental dieting"
that can give you perfect weight control—forever.

By Elsye Birkinshaw

Director and founder, Seminars of Self-Awareness Center
Lecturer, California State University Extension

Published by
Woodbridge Press Publishing Company
Santa Barbara, California 93111

Published and Distributed by
Woodbridge Press Publishing Company
Post Office Box 6189
Santa Barbara, California 93111

Library of Congress Catalog Card Number: 76-16447
International Standard Book Number: 0-912800-23-2

Published simultaneously in the United States and Canada
Printed in the United States of America

Contents

Guide To the 'Mental Diet' Plan

Chapter 1

Introduction:
Prisoner of Your Mind

You are a prisoner of your mind! Your mind keeps you a prisoner as closely confined as if you were behind iron bars. Unbelievable? You can prove it to yourself right now.

What has been your experience with dieting, for example? Are you a "yo-yo" dieter? Have you been successful in losing weight, only to gain it all back when you go off the diet? Have you made up your mind to shed excess pounds, to have a slender, attractive figure—only to have your good resolutions vanish at the very first temptation from some irresistible goodie? Or, have you been saying for years that you should lose weight, but have never been able to summon the will power to make a start? Or, have you been fat from childhood, and never been able to lose weight at all?

If you see yourself in any of these situations, then you will agree that to some extent you are indeed a prisoner of your mind.

But do not despair. A method has been developed to help you to release yourself from this "prison," and for the rest of your life you can have the ideal body you have always wanted, without using a great deal of effort, and without using any will power at all!

Steps to a new image

The only requisite is that you follow the sequence of steps outlined in this book, and that you *persist—even if you do not wholeheartedly believe!*

The objective is for you, yourself, to "program" your subconscious mind. You may now have within your mind a "fat" image of yourself. This plan will help you to replace that with a "slim" image. It is not even necessary for you to have an active belief that this is possible. Reprograming your subconscious mind is as if you were erasing a tape in your tape recorder. You merely play over the first message with a new message and that simple action erases the old while it records the new. So it is, in a manner of speaking, with your subconscious mind.

The method outlined in this book will help you to erase all of the false information with which your mind has been programed since infancy: false information such as, "You are doomed to have weight problems the rest of your life"; or, "You can never hope to have a youthful, slender body with excellent muscle tone." Humbug!

We have proven in our university classes on "mental diet" that even persons who have never been slim in their entire lives have been able to lose weight, without gaining it back, and absolutely without using will power—as long as they *follow the sequence of steps in the plan.* This method is like most things—you get out of it exactly what you put into it; no more, no less!

At this point you may be asking yourself, "What is this miracle?" Let me assure you that it is not a miracle; it is not even very difficult. In fact, it is very simple. It is so simple that at first it may seem unbelievable that it could work; but work it does, as has been proven with hundreds of students in the mental diet classes.

A mental battle

The first thing you must realize is that a mental battle is begun the moment a person goes on a diet. The will is pitted against early childhood conditioning (or "programing") of the subconscious mind, but the moment a person stops using will power the childhood programing always takes over. Obviously, it is impossible to use will power every minute of every day for months and years. That is why, as soon as you go off a diet, you begin to gain back what you have lost. In fact, you often gain more weight than you lost, because your subconscious mind (with its childhood programing) feels deprived and decides to make up for the time lost in dieting.

It sounds almost as if you have a force inside of you that cannot be controlled, doesn't it? But this is not so. The only reason your subconscious mind has not been controlled up to this time is that the correct method of control has not been used. Only within the past few years has any systematic knowledge of the inward working of the mind been developed. We have sent men to the moon, but of the world within us, little has been known. Now a method has been developed to bring your subconscious mind under control, so that you can have the *ideal* body you have always desired.

Childhood programing

To have an understanding of why your subconscious mind is programed (or conditioned) as it is, we must go back to your early childhood. In other words: "How you became the person you are today." That programing is directly related to your weight problem! This exploration of childhood programing will also explain why, even when at times you firmly make up your mind to do certain things, you find yourself unable to do them; or, sometimes, you even do the opposite of the thing you wanted to do.

Most psychologists agree that your character traits were well set by the time you were four, five, or—at the most—six years of age; unless you had a very traumatic experience such as the death of a parent.

Thus, as a yound child, your subconscious mind was conditioned (or programed) by everyone around you: parents, grandparents, aunts, uncles, brothers, sisters, teachers, and friends. You had virtually nothing to say about this, because at that age you had little of the critical faculty within your subconscious that would have enabled you to shield yourself against some of the programing.

As an adult you have more of this critical faculty. If you do not wish to believe something, you can say, either aloud or to yourself, "I do not believe that." Then it does not become programed as a truth in your subconscious mind.

Small children do not have much of this critical faculty because they have little past experience to relate to. So, as a child, you had little choice but to accept everything said to you—as truths. If you have tried to joke with a two- or three-year-old child, you probably have realized that the child tends to accept everything you tell him as truth.

Through the eyes of the child

So it was with you. These early "truths" became the programing with which you have been living from your earliest years until now. Thus, you have probably been trying to relate to your weight problems through the eyes of a two-year-old. Is it any wonder you have had problems in shedding weight?

You can understand the power of this conditioning when you realize that much of it occured through having fun times connected with food: picnics, parties, carnivals, or family outings. Or perhaps your parents told you, time after time, "Finish everything on your plate so you'll grow big." Or, "Clean up your plate; remember the poor children in China."

One of my students told a story of programing she had experienced as a small child. In one of our relaxation periods, she suddenly had a mental picture of herself as a very small child. She had always worn hand-me-down clothes from an older sister. Never had she had a new dress of her very own. To have such a dress had become an obsession. She clearly remembered thinking to herself, "If I were fat I would not have to wear my sister's clothes. I could have my very own new dress." So what happened from that moment on? She started gaining weight and continued to gain weight through her teens and into adulthood. Of course, she did accomplish her goal! She got her very own new dresses—in a very large size!

The moment she became aware of how she, herself, had started this problem, she realized that, in her subconscious mind, she was still looking at life through the eyes of a four-year-old child. She was then able to reprogram her mind successfully; not only losing the weight she wanted to lose, but also maintaining her desired weight without effort.

You must now ask yourself, "How was I programed as a child? Were fun times associated with food—picnics, carnivals, parties? Was I told to clean up my plate, regardless of how full I was? Did my parents think a 'fat' baby was a healthy baby; and, therefore, try to fatten me up?" Take a good, honest, look into your childhood and attempt to "replay" all the experiences, attitudes, feelings, and opinions associated with food by your family and everyone else around you as a child. Did your parents use food as an escape when things were tough? Was it a symbol of prosperity when things were good? Whatever *their* attitudes were are now, very likely, *yours* because bad food habits usually originate with the family.

Most doctors now agree that there is much more to losing weight than just going on a 500- or 1000-calorie diet. There are emotional aspects, escape mechanisms, feelings of inadequacy, feelings of loneliness, or not being loved.

All of these emotions and feelings stem from your early childhood subconscious programing—how you were *taught*. Those early "negative" actions and attitudes of people around you still influence you, greatly.

A first step

The first step in reprograming your subconscious mind is to *write down* all that you can remember regarding food—from as far back in your childhood as you can.

You can make some notes right here:

Chapter 2

Prisoner,
Release Yourself

You, and you alone, can release yourself from the prison of your mind. You must do it by "experiencing," not just by reading. The "tools" or methods, in this book must be experienced; you, and only you, can build the experience in your mind.

Because this book deals with a mind function—something that cannot be seen, heard, tasted, felt or touched—many people fall by the wayside because they feel they must have concrete, material things to work with; for example, weight-loss pills, weight-reducing shots, diets, etc. All of these things may help for a time, but whenever they are stopped the mind once again takes over and you are right back where you started.

So it is very important to accept the concept of "mind-effectiveness" so that we can work with the cause of weight problems—not just the symptoms.

Lost identity

The first premise we must recognize is that most people, especially those who are a great deal overweight and those who have an involuntary compulsion for food, have lost identity with themselves. They no longer like themselves, or respect themselves, and food is substituted as "a way of life" to make up for all the loneliness, the good times they have missed—the times when they feel or have felt completely alone and unloved. Food has become a kind of "god," one which they must incessantly feed. If only the enjoyment of eating were everlasting! Unfortunately, it lasts for only a short time; then the compulsion begins all over again. For many people, this way of life becomes a hell on earth!

A power within

It is sad that such persons do not realize that the power to end this misery lies within themselves. Each of us has within his head a "billion-dollar computer," waiting and ready to be used—*the mind!*

It waits only for us to recognize and be aware of it. This is the great secret. You must become aware that you have this great mind power, the ability to choose to do, or be, whatever you wish. Outside circumstances, no matter what they may be, have no power over you. *You* have all the power within yourself; but you, and only you, can become aware of it and let it work for you.

Do you realize what this means? It means that the moment you become aware of the power of your "billion-dollar computer," you can transform the compulsion for food to an irresistible desire for a beautiful, slim, youthful body! But—and this is the secret—only *you* can do this. No one else on the face of this earth, whether it be doctor, minister, friends, spouse or children, can ever make you do it. *You must do it yourself!*

At this point I know you are saying, "But how can I believe in and use something inside myself that I have never seen, heard, tasted or touched?" Here is the beauty of this whole new concept: you have only to start using the "tools," or methods, and in a very short time (sometimes only 21 days) you *will* begin to believe! The moment you come to believe, your weight problem is over!

Six simple "tools" to use

So now, this very instant, begin to regain the identity with yourself that you have lost over the years. Use your creative imagination, and picture to yourself an image of the way you would like to look. See yourself with the ideal body—energetic, youthful, slim, agile, strong, and full of vitality. You can attain this ideal body, you can realize your ideal body image by using the "tools" in this book.

Six simple "tools," or methods have recently been discovered in studies of the mind that, used in proper sequence, will work miracles for you. You will not only be able to shed the excess weight, you will have your ideal body image for a lifetime without ever again having to use "will power." The processes for maintaining your ideal weight will be established in your subconscious mind as firmly as any other involuntary bodily process, such as your heartbeat. Your subconscious mind will take over the job of maintaining your weight as it now controls your breathing. You never have to say to yourself, "I took a breath 20 seconds ago, it is time to take another breath!" Your breathing is automatic. As soon as you establish the subconscious programing of food patterns, that, too, will be automatic. You will never have to take conscious thought of how much food to eat, how many calories you've had for the day, how much exercise to take. Your subconscious mind will take over the control of these things.

The majority of my students have found that, as soon as the subconscious programing is completed, they no longer have food "temptations." At party times they have no desire to eat or drink any more than is necessary to maintain their ideal body image.

One of these students previously had never been able to resist Danish apple turnovers—her favorite food "temptation." One week after attending the mental diet class, she was offered some apple turnovers during a coffee break. She tried to eat one, she said, but absolutely could not force herself to take even a bite.

This is an example of how subconscious programing works. As soon as the programing is completed, you no longer have to use will power. Your mind controls your appetite and you cannot eat when you should not eat.

A "law" of nature

When you begin to use the six "mind tools" I refered to, you are putting into motion a basic law of the mind. This law works as other laws of nature work—laws such as the law of gravity, or the "law" that says, "water always seeks its own level," or the simple mathematical rule of $2+2 = 4$. These "laws" always work in the same way—*and they always work!*

So, if you put into motion the "law" of the mind by using the six tools, you *always* attain your goals. Set a weight "goal" of losing 30 to 40 pounds, or more, and you *will* lose it. It can happen no other way—because, at this moment, you have within yourself the power to make it happen. You have only to start.

20 lbs

What are the six "mind" tools?

The first tool is to "Know Yourself." You need self-knowledge—you must know the reasons you over-eat. You must be mercilessly honest with yourself.

The second tool consists of "Setting a Goal." Your "goal" *weight,* of course. There are specific ways to do this, explained in detail in Chapter 4.

The third tool is your "Creative Imagination." You must learn to use your creative imagination. Your mind thinks in pictures, not in words. Try this little experiment right now: recall what you had for breakfast this morning. What do you see in your mind's eye? Do you see the sentence, "I had scrambled eggs?" or do you see a *plate* with scrambled eggs on it? Your mind sees images. It is important to develop you creative mental ability. Everyone has it but in all probability it has been allowed to lie dormant. This is also discussed in detail in Chapter 4. Here, too, there are specific ways to develop creative imagination.

The fourth tool consists of the "Mirror Technique." Now you are ready to actually begin your subconscious programing! This technique will erase a major part of the negative programing which has been firmly set into your mind up to this time. The mirror technique is a method for raising your self-image—the basis of all subconscious programing, as you will see in Chapter 5.

The fifth tool is "Words of Power." These are affirmations or statements to yourself that will induce positive programing instead of the negative programing you now have!

The sixth and most important tool is "Relaxation." This is a *must*, because relaxation is an imperative condition for reaching your subconscious mind. There is no other way. It is something that most people must learn, just as they must learn how to swim. We are not born with the capacity for deliberate relaxation. We must consciously learn how.

An input of information

Another *must* in subconscious programing is to input data, or information, to your mind, so your mind can make correct decisions. More specifically, you will now put into your mind positive information, in place of the negative information with which you formerly were programed. You must also know how your body relates to your mind and how the body responds to the dictates of your subconscious mind.

For example, your feeling of hunger is controlled by what may be called your "appestat," a nerve complex associated with the hypothalmus which is located at the base of the brain. The appestat is controlled, in part, by your level of blood sugar. If your blood sugar level is low, a "let's eat" chemistry will be stimulated and a brain cell impression is "fired up" for hunger. We all know how it feels to be hungry. So we just duplicate the brain cell patterns we've had since we were born and the body reacts in the same way it always does. The stomach growls, digestive juices begin to flow, salivation begins, and you feel hunger pangs.

An example of wrong "programing"

Let's see what happens when we follow the instructions of this mind control center that has been wrongly programed. It is 3:00 P.M., you've had a good lunch, and dinner isn't for several hours. Your subconscious programing tells you that a cup of coffee and a candy bar will make you feel better and give you more energy. The candy bar is largely sugar. The sugar is absorbed quickly into the blood stream and reaches your appestat control center which sends out an "I'm full" signal. This control center reacts to the high blood sugar level, and "shuts off" the body chemistry that produces a "hunger" feeling. This would be just fine except for one thing: when you eat sugar the complex reactions eventually cause the blood sugar level to again become drastically lower—perhaps long before dinner time. You are ravenously hungry. Your appestat now says, "I'm starving." This is the way your nervous system works with wrong programing, leading to wrong responses.

An example of good "programing"

Now let's reconstruct this situation with the right programing and see what happens. You have reprogramed your subconscious mind with facts about food, about calories, sugars, proteins, etc. Now when you have that feeling of hunger at 3:00 P.M., you may eat; but, instead of sweets, you eat protein. This works, as the candy bar did, to raise the level of your blood sugar. But, it also helps to keep it at a higher level, possibly until shortly before dinner time. Then, at dinner you eat only your normal amount of food.

At mealtime there is a good way of using your appestat to shut off that "I'm hungry" feeling before you eat too much. That is to chew your food thoroughly and to eat slowly. You have heard this all of your life, but have you ever known why it helps you to lose weight? It takes some *20 minutes* for a higher blood sugar level to reach your appestat in order to turn on the "I'm full" signal. So, if you eat rapidly you may, by the time the signal is perceived, have eaten much more than is needed. Eat more slowly, chew your food thoroughly, and your appestat can turn off your appetite before you have overeaten.

Ways to control your "appetite control"

There are several ways, then, to help "set" your appestat at a normal level:

1. If you eat between meals, eat protein foods such as cheese, egg, meat.

2. Eat slowly and chew each mouthful thoroughly so that when the "I'm full" message reaches your appestat, you will not have eaten too much.

3. If you must nibble on something between meals, make it something chewy or crunchy—such as celery, carrots, or hard cheese. Even sunflower seeds are good!

4. Learn to eat natural, nutritious, high-vitamin/mineral foods.

5. Eat concentrated foods that provide nourishment without adding pounds.

Diet supplements are important

All "foods" are not nutritious, so it is important to take some kind of vitamin-mineral supplement with this program. Many of our foods are lacking in trace elements that should come from the soil. A few years ago, it was found that the death rate from heart attacks in nine northern Georgia counties was double that of nine counties in the south. Research showed that this apparently was due to a lack of certain trace elements in the northern Georgia soil.

In my judgment, *it is necessary to take a natural vitamin-mineral supplement.* (Do not take the vitamins made synthetically.) It was shown experimentally that rats fed synthetic vitamins had less energy than rats fed natural vitamins. Their hair was duller and they had a shorter lifespan than another group fed natural vitamins.

One warning about your appestat: once it is "set" at a normal level, which will keep you at your ideal weight, it can be upset by either sugar or alcohol. Both of these interfere with the signal system of the appestat. Sugar craves more sugar and alcohol craves more alcohol!

So you can see, there is much more than we had once supposed to losing weight and keeping it off. Successful dieting is primarily the result of a mental attitude. The subconscious mind controls all of the involuntary bodily functions, so if you control your subconscious mind, your subconscious mind will control your weight problem for the rest of your life!

"Empty" foods are damaging

There is still more information to be "input" to your mind. For example, you must learn what the effects of empty carbohydrates are on your body. When you throw empty carbohydrates into your body, you "choke" its metabolism. The body does not know what else to do with an excess of "foodless" starches and sweets, so it simply "dumps" them in the form of excess body fat. That's why over-refined, empty carbohydrates are great troublemakers. If the two chief offenders, white flour products and white sugar products, were taken off the market, there would be a tremendous improvement in health and vitality of many people. As much as 80 percent of their excess body weight would be shed.

This doesn't mean you should not eat any carbohydrates. You can eat any of the whole grain breads or rolls, cereals, or rice. The chief function of carbohydrates is to aid in providing some energy for the body and to assist in the digestion and assimilation of other foods. In moderation, they are very important to metabolism. However, most people eat far too much of them. They are stored as excess fat. When the body finally breaks them down, the carbohydrates eventually form pyruvic acid, which not only inhibits the disposal of body fat, but is actually converted into more fat. Another objection to too many carbohydrates is that they can cause vitamin deficiencies; because, in an effort to burn up the excess carbohydrates, the body uses extra B vitamins. This can result in a B-vitamin shortage for other bodily functions.

If you never again even taste refined white sugar you will still get enough sugar for your body needs by eating fresh fruits and vegetables. All breads, cereals, and other starchy vegetables are changed into sugar in the process of digestion. In fact, about 65 percent of the food you eat is transformed into sugar.

A story is told about an Englishman who lived during the 1800s. He was short (5'5"); and very fat, about 350 pounds. He was miserable, and so fat he couldn't even see his feet. He was frantic. He went to one doctor after another; they all told him he was eating too much, which he already knew—so the advice didn't really make him happy. The doctors put him on low-calorie diets which made him even more miserable. By the merest chance, he happened to go to an ear surgeon who had discovered a strange thing about foods. (He was losing his hearing in addition to all of his other problems.) After the ear surgeon had his hearing problems under control, he put him on a diet different from any other he had ever had. In less than a year he had lost 50 pounds and 12 inches around the middle. This was his diet!

For breakfast: 4 ounces of either beef, fish, liver, or bacon; one slice of toast; and coffee with no sugar.

For lunch: 5 ounces fish or meat (no pork—any kind of poultry); choice of any vegetable (except potatoes); 1 slice of whole wheat bread; fruit for dessert; and 1 glass of sherry or Madeira wine (no beer, champagne, or hard liquor), the wine containing some digestive enzymes.

For afternoon break: 2 or 3 ounces of fresh fruit; 1 slice of toast; coffee.

For dinner: same as lunch.

Before bed: 1 glass of wine.

Why did this diet allow this man to lose weight when it contains so many calories? The reason, of course, is *low carbohydrates*. The troublemakers are usually carbohydrates. The body just can't handle them in very large quantity.

The overweight syndrome is a by-product of our

way of life. We all love sweet things; therefore, many of our foods contain added sugar. Even some meats have sugar added in commercial processing. Check the label on a package of hot dogs, for example.

To make a point, I asked a student what she usually prepared for a family picnic. What were the foods her family asked for? Her reply: hot dogs, soda water, watermelon, potato salad, marshmallows, and so on and on. All of these contain sugar and other carbohydrates, but are rather low in other nutritional elements. Picnics may be a lot of fun for the family, but dietwise they are often disasters.

New attitudes toward eating

Considering all we have discussed in this chapter, doesn't it seem just pure logic to take control of the subconscious mind and create a new set of rules and attitudes toward your eating habits?

Begin by dissolving the old negative habits and attitudes, and by establishing new positive habits and attitudes toward food. You may wonder what attitudes and emotions have to do with losing weight, but it has been found that negative emotions set up a vicious circle, and that circle must be broken. For instance, if you have a resentment toward someone, it creates negative feelings within your mind; and, many times, in a reaction to the irritability, you eat!

A student told our class that previously, when she came home from work each night, she headed straight for the refrigerator and ate anything that was there. When she heard that feelings of resentment and ir- ritability often triggered the appetite, she took a long hard look at her attitudes toward her job and her boss. That was the answer. Each day many things happened at work that generated negative emotions within her. Her boss had an irritating way of not listening to her; of walking away in the middle of a suggestion she was making. Every day there was some new irritation.

She compensated for her negative feelings by eat- ing. Somehow this seemed to make her feel much bet- ter. The problem was, after a year of raiding the refrigerator each night after work, she didn't *look* much better.

At this point she realized that she had to change her attitudes toward her boss and her job. She came to realize that she had the power of control within herself, in her subconscious mind, that would com- pletely change the situation. That is just what hap- pened!

After about three weeks of raising her self-image, she found her boss no longer irritated her. Strangely enough, her boss gradually changed his attitude toward her and accepted many of her suggestions.

The best thing of all was that she no longer had an obsessive craving for food and thus was able to lose her excess weight in a short time.

By the use of positive suggestion and by cultivat- ing happy, positive emotions and attitudes, the sub- conscious mind can be programed to take control of the carbohydrate- and fat-storing functions of your body to help bring your metabolism into balance.

So why not dissolve the old negative attitudes and begin now to establish new and positive attitudes? When you have totally positive attitudes, you avoid much of the stress and anxiety of life. Worries and boredom will vanish and inferiority complexes will fail to influence and control you. You will feel the desire for creativity and self-expression. This will reach into all areas of your life; yes, even your love life will improve!

Chapter 3

Know Thyself

Do you know yourself? Do you know why you crave strawberry sundaes with mounds of whipped cream, or double-thick malted milkshakes? Or why, after a three-course meal, you are feeling hunger pangs within an hour? Do you know why you get that empty, gnawing feeling just before going to bed, or while watching television? If you did know why, you would not be reading this book, and you would not have a weight problem.

Most doctors agree that there is a maze of emotional problems involved in obesity. Fat people have a fat "image" of themselves, in their minds—usually much worse than the reality. In certain experiments fat people have been asked to pick a likeness of themselves from among several pictures. They usually select a picture of someone much fatter than themselves. They have a poor self-image. In fact, their self-image is often so poor that they think, "What's the use?" So they never start any weight loss plan. They feel sure it won't work—before even trying.

A new "mental diet" plan

The beautiful simplicity of the tools outlined in the "mental diet" plan in this book helps such people to realize that there is hope. This plan helps them to understand the great part the mind plays in the situation; and, by understanding this, and realizing they have control over their minds, the weight problem can be solved.

Overweight people rarely eat just to feed their bodies. They usually eat to feed emotional cravings of which they are aware only vaguely—if at all. These emotional cravings started when they were children. They can be due to one thing or to a combination of several things: for example, not enough love as a child, or outright rejection as a child.

Excess weight can even be used as a "protective armor." If a girl is afraid of men (perhaps because she was mistreated by a male in her childhood), she may let herself get fat for protection. After all, what man is interested in a fat girl?

A *classic example*

Another student related just such a problem. She grew up feeling that her father was disappointed that she had not been born a boy. Consequently her feelings of self-worth were very limited. Perceiving no circumstances to the contrary she was always ready to accept the blame when things went wrong, and came to feel that this was her destiny.

She felt that work demands on her were so excessive that she needed to develop some defense—and this turned out to be putting on weight, so that she could not be expected to do so much, a technique that seemed to accomplish its purpose. But it did create other problems.

Strange as it may seem she did not eat very much more than the other children, but all of her food seemed to go to fat. When she was so very fat, it somehow seemed justified that she should be rejected: after all, who could possibly love such a fat girl? The food also seemed to make up for the lack of love in her life.

This student had a very difficult time developing a feeling of self-worth. She had to work constantly to realize that, as much as anyone, she had a right to have a youthful, slender, beautiful body. She had to work to overcome her fear of men, because subconsciously she was afraid that if she did become slender, a man would be attracted to her. Although she was afraid of this, she also desired it.

Here was a deep-seated conflict. Before it could be

resolved it had to be faced. She had to build inner courage and lift up her self-image before she could attain her ideal body image.

This girl's case was unusual. Most people do not have problems so deeply rooted. However, the "happy ending" was that as soon as she uplifted her self-image so that she felt worthy of being beautiful, she was able to lose weight—and to lose her fear of men at the same time. When the class was over, she was well on her way to becoming a beautiful young woman.

Awareness is the key

You must become aware of your particular emotional problems. Awareness is three-fourths of the battle. Once you become aware of why you react as you do to food, it becomes a simple matter to use the tools outlined in this book to erase the negative emotions that cause the problem.

Most students become aware of their hangups during the relaxation period that is a fundamental part of the "mental diet" plan. One student, who was very much overweight, realized that his problem had been an overindulgent mother, who not only believed that a fat baby was a healthy baby, but also soothed away all his childish hurts and problems with generous servings of the most rich and fattening foods. When he was very, very good, he also was rewarded with his favorite meal: double portions of such goodies as mounds of whipped potatoes oozing with melted butter, corn-on-the-cob; and, for dessert, delicious pie heaped with whipped cream. He had to reprogram his subconscious mind with the knowledge that a true reward is having an ideal body, energized with vitality, agility, and strength.

Another student, also substantially overweight, said she suddenly had a flashback during her relaxation period. She saw herself as a young child, shouting in anger at her thin aunt, whom she much disliked: "When I grow up, I won't even look like you. I'll be big and fat." And so she was! She, herself, had programed her subconscious mind at a tender age to act and look the exact opposite of her aunt who, unfortunately, happened to be very thin. As soon as the student became aware of this, she was able to begin the necessary subconscious reprograming; and, for the first time in her life, was able to lose weight and keep it off.

Flashes of insight

Many times, then, an overweight problem is a form of rebellion. As you learn to relax, you will begin to have flashes of insight wherein you will see exactly why you've been having weight problems your whole life.

Your mind is self-regulating and self-protecting. By that I mean that until you have the inner strength and courage to face your emotions, your subconscious mind will protect you and will not allow a particular emotional hangup to surface, so that you can become aware of it.

One of my students worked very hard trying to learn why she had a weight problem; but, for quite some time, was unable to achieve the necessary insight. She persisted, however, in raising her self-image and also in developing inner courage. One day she asked to speak to me privately. She told me that at last she had discovered her problem. Her subconscious mind had used obesity as a form of protection. As a young girl, she had the traumatic experience of being molested. Her subconscious mind had not let her remember that incident until she had the inner strength to face it and cope with it. She had not been able to remember it at all since the time it had oc-cured, when she was a small child. Finally, when she had the inner courage, her mind let her recall it and she was at last able to realize how she had used "fat" as an armor or protection to avoid a similar ex-perience.

You can control

This is one of the great discoveries of mind research, that *you* can be *in control* of each and every situation. As soon as you become aware, in your con-scious mind, the battle is won; and *you are no longer a prisoner of your mind!*

Through the process of relaxation, you find that

you are the cause of your overweight problem because of your own subconscious programing. You are the *cause*, and the *effects* are *fat!* The secret of success in this method of losing weight and gaining an ideal body image is to realize not only that you are the cause, but also that you can reverse the processes that made you overweight. In reversing the processes, you are still the *cause*, but now the *effect* is the materialization of your *ideal body image*—an ideal body that is full of vitality, agility, and vibrant health—yours for life! You have programed your ideal body image in your subconscious mind and it is now a determinant in the development of your body.

The body obeys the mind

The body "obeys" the dictates of the mind. This has been demonstrated in an experiment in subliminal perception through the medium of motion pictures. In the experiment, a suggestion was flashed on the screen instructing the viewers to go to the lobby during the intermisssion and buy popcorn and cola. The viewers did not consciously know that such a suggestion had been made to them, because the message flashed across the screen so rapidly it was not discernible to the eye; therefore, it did not register consciously in the mind. Nevertheless, there was a significant increase in the sales of the items suggested!

A similar thing happens when a person is hypnotized. The conscious mind is bypassed and a suggestion is entered directly into the subconscious mind. It has been demonstrated that a person under hypnosis, told that a pencil touching his arm is a glowing cigarette, may actually develop a blister on the arm.

This same kind of thing happened to you as a very young child. You were "hypnotized" by everyone around you—parents, grandparents, friends, sisters, brothers, and even by yourself, as was observed in the story above about the thin grandmother.

This is what we mean by subconscious programing. As a child you tended to believe everything that was told to you, because at that age you did not have what we call a "critical faculty" in your subconscious mind to screen out things you did not want to believe. For example, a young child who hears a parent say that he is a "bad" child, may misinterpret or exaggerate it to the point where he believes he is a creature not worthy to live.

Because you tended to believe everything you were told as a small child, much "emotional garbage" has already been programed. We call it "emotional garbage" because most of it is negative and gives rise to feelings of depression, not feeling loved, not having a feeling of self-worth. This is all "garbage"—destructive lies. The truth about you is that you are a being of tremendous creativity and power, both of which may at this moment be dormant within you.

Is it any wonder that you are a prisoner of your mind? Someone, during your childhood, put you in that prison, but *you* have the key to unlock the door and start using your tremendous powers.

No condemnation

A first step is to stop condemning yourself, stop blaming yourself for your shortcomings, stop blaming yourself for your errors. You are not responsible for these negative feelings lodged in your subconscious mind. You were "hypnotized" into believing them when you were a child. However, if you do nothing about them after you have become aware of them, you will have to take the responsibility from that moment on. Because only you can do anything about yourself and your mind.

Control your mind and your mind will control your body and make it into the ideal body you have always wanted.

A checklist of reasons

An effective thing you can do to accomplish this is to make a list of all the things you think may be reasons for your weight problem. Be honest with yourself. On the next page are listed the most common reasons. Check each one you think may be a factor contributing to your overweight problem. If there are others, not listed, add them at the bottom.

1. False hunger (after three good meals, you still have that "gnawing").

2. T.V. or "just-before-bedtime" nibbling.

3. Compulsive finishing of leftovers.

4. Not enough exercise.

5. Alcohol or sweets.

6. Too many artificial foods, such as gravies, sauces, pastries or sandwiches.

7. Eating because of feelings of loneliness, not being loved, or as an escape mechanism.

8. Sequence of meals in wrong order, such as no breakfast, light lunch, heavy dinner.

9. Do you usually eat and run, not taking time to really taste your food?

10. Do you diet without taking vitamin-mineral supplements?

11. Glandular disorder, such as low blood sugar, thyroid, etc.

12. List any reasons not listed above:

Eat wrong foods to prove my independence.

Some of writing is not mine

A closer look

Here, then, in this analysis is a valuable first tool in your effort to know yourself and the reasons for a weight problem. Let's elaborate on this list of reasons why people overeat.

1. *False hunger.* Because much of our food today is devitalized, you may have to consume many extra pounds of food to satisfy your body's need and craving for vitamins and minerals. For example, white bread does not satisfy as much as whole wheat bread. Food experiments on animals have revealed that animals, like humans, experience false hunger with devitalized food and consume more in order to satisfy body cravings. A student told us he had been reared on white bread and often ate as much as six slices of toast at breakfast. Usually, two hours later he was famished. After he began taking natural vitamin and mineral supplements, he was satisfied with one piece of toast and did not get hungry until lunch.

2. *T.V. or "just-before-bedtime" nibbling.* If you have a compulsion to nibble, try raw vegetables or nuts instead of potato chips or pretzels. One student craved the sensation of chewing rather than actual food, so she started snacking on carrots instead of potato chips, and began losing unwanted weight.

3. *Compulsion to finish leftovers.* If you cannot bear to see food wasted and you must eat the remain-

ders whether or not you are hungry, it is probably be-cause you were programed as a child to "think of the poor starving children." One of my students solved the problem by getting a dog to eat the leftovers!

4. *Not enough exercise.* We seem to have become a nation of sitters: sitting at desks, in cars, in front of the T.V., and in stadiums and theatres. We don't get enough exercise.

Sometimes your muscles are crying to be exercised and the feeling is misinterpreted to mean that you are hungry. You go to the refrigerator for snacks and this dulls the cry of the muscles. Shortly your feelings of "hunger" are dulled—and your muscles are also fooled into believing they craved food.

Interestingly enough, being thirsty can some-times by misinterpreted as being hungry. A student told our class that drinking a glass of club soda (without the booze!) had really helped control her ap-petite. For years, she said, she had believed that she was hungry at certain times when in reality she was just thirsty. Keep some low-calorie drinks in your refrigerator. If you feel hunger pangs, try drinking something instead of eating. You'll be surprised to discover that "9 times out of 10" you are no longer hungry.

Exercise does not need to be dull sit-ups and knee-bends. Recent research has shown that because a muscle can grow only at a certain rate, it needs only a small amount of the *right* exercise to tone it up and keep it firm.

Six-Second Exercises

Here are several exercises that can keep your muscles in good tone without requiring more than a few minutes a day:

A. *Towel exercise.* After your daily bath or shower, take your towel and loop it behind your neck. Pull in your chin, and pull on both ends of the towel, resisting with your neck for just six seconds. Now slide the towel down to small of the back. Again pull forward on the towel and resist the counteraction with the muscles in the buttocks and the stomach muscles. Now loop the towel under your toes, and pull up with both hands while your toes push down. Again hold for six seconds. Repeat once on each foot and you are done for the day.

B. *Abdominal corset exercise.* If you have time for only one exercise do not miss the abdominal corset exercise. The autonomic nervous system involves all your abdominal organs. It is very important to keep the muscles in that region of your body in good tone.

Exercise was just what one of my students

needed. She had a reasonably good shape, but her abdominal region had been sadly neglected. Her stomach muscles bulged, and she looked as if she were about five months pregnant. After she had done the abdominal corset exercise for about three weeks, she found to her delight that not only did her stomach muscles become firm but also that her "tummy" was *flat*. Her posture was also much better. She corrected sagging shoulders; and, strangely enough, even her face looked much better because with the better posture her double chin had disappeared.

A strong muscular "corset" supports all of the vital organs in the abdominal area. If, once a day, you bring this "corset" into a firm, muscular contraction, holding it for 6 seconds, the strength of these muscles will rapidly increase.

So once a day, tense your abdominal muscles (try to "touch your spine" with them), hold for 6 seconds, then relax. Research has shown that one such contraction performed once a day makes the muscles 6 percent stronger in one week, and 66 percent stronger in 11 weeks. Just this one exercise will help to save your waistline. It will also help to save your posture, avoid sagging shoulders, and "middle age spread."

C. *Jump rope exercise.* One of the best all-around exercises is the childhood sport of "jump rope." One student was a beautiful young woman, but she had sadly neglected her body. She was in general very well-proportioned, but her muscles were flabby, her stomach protruded, and she was substantially overweight. At the time she was taking the class, she was having traumatic problems at home; and, consequently, seemed unable to stay on the diet. However, she did do her mental programing and also jumped rope. By the time the class was completed, without any dieting whatsoever, she had lost weight and firmed up her muscles merely by jumping rope. If you use this exercise, start by doing 25 jumps the first day, 50 the second and third days, working up eventually to 200 jumps per day. This assumes, of course, that you are generally in good health. You do not even need a rope; just let your arms and hands move as if you had a rope in your hands.

5. *Alcohol and sweets.* "Non-natural" sweets are "foods" highest in calories and lowest in general nutrition. They pervert the appetite by causing a craving for more sweets. Try a low-calorie drink when you crave sweets. If that does not help and your craving is extreme, try some of the special candies made without sugar especially for people who cannot tolerate sweets.

Alcohol is a high-calorie food. It can also overstimulate the appetite. After having two or three drinks, a person often imagines that he is ravenously hungry.

6. *Too many artificial foods.* If you have a craving for rich desserts, cakes, pies, thick sauces, or even certain sandwiches, keep in mind that nature itself does not produce these and you do not get much nutrition from them. Nature *does* produce delicious fruits and salad vegetables, both of which are low in calories and rich in nutrients.

7. *Eating because of feelings of loneliness.* Many people eat as an escape from disagreeable life situations. We heard one member of our class report that she ate because, for several serious reasons, she had a very unstable home life. She never knew if her husband would be in a pleasant or unpleasant mood; and, because her own feelings were rather unstable, she ate to escape the total situation. Another student said he ate to escape a nagging

mother. Still another, a very shy young man, said he ate because he was lonely, felt unloved, without friends or family in a strange city. A girl disliked her job intensely, and overate for consolation as soon as she got home from work. A young man had a different outlook on food. He considered rich food a sign of prosperity, because he had been very poor as a child. So he ate to make up for childhood cravings. Usually, if such problems are solved, or even lessened, overeating is also considerably lessened. It has been found that a hobby or sport of some kind can help to substitute for overeating.

8. *Wrong sequence of meals and foods.* It is known that a hot, thin soup at the beginning of a meal actually stimulates your appetite. However, salad served first fills you with nutritious food and dulls an overactive appetite. The common habit of no breakfast, medium lunch, and a heavy dinner often causes problems. One student said she had been brought up in a family whose habit was to eat a big breakfast, the main meal in the middle of the day, and a light snack in the evening. None of the family ever had a weight problem. After she married, however, the main meal was at night when her husband came home from work. She soon noticed that she was putting on weight. She changed this sequence of eating and lost the excess weight.

9. *Eat-and-run habit.* Take more time with your

meals. Not only will you be more relaxed, you will also get more nutrition from your food. If you chew everything twice as long, you will not only crave less food, you will also satisfy your taste buds and your craving for chewing. There is also a physiological reason for a more leisurely pace at meals; as mentioned earlier, it takes 20 minutes for your appestat to get a signal from the rise in the level of your blood sugar in order to send out your "I'm full" signal.

10. *Vitamin and mineral supplements.* Vitamin-mineral supplementation is a *must*, in my judgment, even when you are not on a diet. Why? Certain things, such as overcooking, destroy vitamins, and there are certain disorders that interfere with your body's ability to utilize good foods. A few of these are: infections, ulcers, colitis, diarrhea, smoking (destroys vitamin C), aspirin (destroys vitamin C), alcohol (destroys thiamine), sugar (destroys thiamine), antacids (destroy vitamin B), excessive sweating (destroys vitamin B).

These are just a few of the things that destroy food values or reduce your body's ability to utilize nutrients. Supplements can help to make up the deficit. Always use the natural vitamins, not the synthetic ones. Experimental feeding of silver foxes with synthetic vitamins resulted in dull fur, loss of energy, and less growth compared with a group fed natural vitamins.

11. *Glandular disorder.* This problem is the exception in obesity rather than the rule! However, we are all aware that a sluggish thyroid prevents proper

utilization of food. If you believe your metabolism is disturbed, it is advisable to see your physician for proper tests and diagnosis.

12. *Listing your reasons.* Your problem will probably be covered in one or more of the above reasons. If it is not, analyze it carefully, and try to come to an understanding of it. Awareness of an overweight problem is three-fourths of the battle in solving it.

Power foods for an ideal body

There are certain foods we call *power* foods because you get a lot of mileage out of your calories. You may utilize some or all of them in your diet. They all have much more nutritional value than most foods, in relation to their calories.

Blackstrap molasses has generous amounts of the B vitamins, calcium, phosphorus, iron, and copper. One tablespoon of this molasses contains as much iron as nine eggs.

Yogurt is of benefit to persons of all ages. It helps the body to manufacture B vitamins and supplies "predigested" protein. Indigestion is helped by yogurt. It also aids in retaining youthful characteristics to a late age.

Liver contains B vitamins, vitamin A, minerals, plus providing antistress vitamins. It supplies energy. In tests on rats, one group fed an ordinary diet swam an average of only 13.3 minutes whereas a liver-fed group swam vigorously for an average of 2 hours.

Sunflower seeds are satisfying as a pickup snack and for regulating your appestat, because of the high protein content. They also have eight minerals, in addition to vitamin B complex and vitamins D and E.

Lecithin should always be taken when on a diet because it helps to prevent a "drawn look" during reducing, retards the aging process, and reduces the cholesterol level in the blood. It is also a natural tranquilizer and rebuilds your body cells.

Brewer's yeast is, indeed, a *power* food as it contains not only a large amount of the vitamin B complex, but also 16 amino acids plus 18 minerals. It is a perfect reducing food because it is low in calories and has almost no fat.

Wheat germ is rich in vitamin E plus the vitamin B complex. Half a cup of raw wheat germ provides the equivalent protein of four eggs.

These *power* foods have a much higher content of vitamins, minerals, amino acids, and nutritional supplements than ordinary foods. They are an excellent value in terms both of money and energy.

It is not necessary to include all of these power foods in your diet; but, as you can see, for each one you do add, you increase your nutritional intake, plus realizing the added bonuses of greater energy, retardation of the aging process, better memory, and a rebuilding of body cells and organs.

Chapter 4

Triggering Your 'Billion-Dollar Computer'

Your "billion dollar computer," your subconscious mind, has a power for weight control that can be activated in only one way: by setting a *goal* and *writing it down*. The goal must be written or you really do not have a firm goal. One of my students thought it was not necessary to write down his weight goal; he thought he could just "think it." But he soon found that he was not really progressing toward this illusive "goal" just "floating" in his mind. Only when he "firmed up" his goal and wrote it down, did he begin to make progress.

You must *use* your mind specifically and concretely or it will not work for you.

At this point, you may be asking, "Why is it necessary to set a goal in order to lose weight? I know very well that I want to lose weight. Why go through

192
150

all this nonsense?" There is a definite answer to your question and a good reason for goal-setting. You are a goal-striver by nature. That is the way all of us are created. Often, when you have a feeling of frustration, without being able to pinpoint the cause, it is probably because you have reached one goal and have not yet set another. A goal helps to provide direction, purpose, and satisfaction.

A goal is a destination

Why bother to set a weight goal? Because it defines your destination—just as you have a destination in mind when you start on your summer vacation. Without such a destination, or goal, in mind you would spend your time aimlessly and get nowhere. So it is in your weight control program. If you do not set a specific goal of weight loss, you will probably never lose even a pound! This is simply the way your mind works.

One student who strongly disbelieved this turned out to be the only member of that class of some 40 students who did not lose a single pound of weight. This experience convinced her that it was necessary to write down her weight goal. She took another class, followed the essential procedures, and made a success of it.

One of the most outstanding experiences in goal accomplishment happened to another student—or rather she made it happen! Some years previously this woman had a gorgeous figure. Her measurements at that time were perfect and so was her weight—she was a strikingly beautiful, statuesque woman. But she went through a tragic divorce, an experience that often leads to feelings of depression and loss of self-esteem. Gradually she allowed the pounds to accumulate until, when she came to our class, she was definitely overweight—quite a contrast to the shapely person she had formerly been—and she was determined to do something about it.

She had tried many of the standard diets. She had lost a few pounds each time and then gained them back as soon as she went off the diet. While in our relaxation period, analyzing her emotional problems, she discovered two things that she knew were at the root of her problem. One—she had lost completely her feeling of self-worth; and, two—she had not set a specific goal and written it down. She worked on these two things, using the "mirror technique" (see Chapter 5) to raise her feeling of self-worth and achieve a much better self-image; then writing down on paper the exact amount she wanted to lose by a certain date.

Her subconscious "computer" then took over, and from that time on, she began to lose weight. By the end of the class, she had lost 20 pounds. Later, she reported that she had lost an additional 25 pounds and was still losing without those terrible feelings of self-deprivation.

Her remarkable transformation was an inspiration to me and a new life for her! It was an outstanding example not only of goal setting, but also of effective subconscious programing.

An important sequence

It is very important to follow the sequence of steps as they are outlined in this book. The first thing you must do, of course, is decide exactly what you want to weigh and how long you want to take to lose the required amount of weight. You must know yourself and realize how long it takes you to lose. The statement, "Know thyself," becomes very important.

You must also do some soul-searching to decide why you "hang on" to food. Is it a "security blanket?" Is it a source of pleasure? Do you eat because you feel lonely or unloved? Exactly why do you overeat? Or why do you crave sweets?

If, as you ask yourself these questions, you are at this time unable to get a clear picture of why you have a food "hang-up," don't be overly concerned. As you learn to relax, you will find that the answers will be relayed from your subconscious mind to your conscious mind. A Japanese-American who had been interned during World War II, discovered that his hang-up with food was directly connected with that experience. He had remembered talking to other children in the camp about all the delicious foods they used to have such as ice cream, candies, etc., before they had been interned, and how they were going to make up for it when they were free again. He did make up for it—for 35 years! As soon as he realized what he was doing, he was able to control his craving for sweets. Awareness is three-fourths of the "fat" battle.

The specific steps of the mental dieting plan must be followed when setting your weight goal, and they must be followed in *exact sequence* or they will not work. The reason is that you are setting into motion a "law," a "law of goals." This law is just as predictable as a mathematical law because, if you follow its precepts, and take the steps in sequence, you will *always* reach your goal.

Set weight goals in stages

It has been found that it is easier to set weight goals in three stages—on a short, medium, and long-range time span. For the first steps, you will decide on your goal for the short-range—the next week to ten days—and specify how much weight you want to lose in that span of time. Next, you will set a medium goal, halfway between your starting time and your final goal weight, which is your long-range goal. Depending on how much you wish to lose, the long-range goal could be as short a time as one month, or as long a time as a year or two. Only you can decide how long you wish to take in losing your excess poundage.

One student set a weight-loss goal of 65 pounds. She knew herself well enough to realize that she had to firmly set a "change-of-food-habit" before her weight would stay off permanently. Also, she had to get rid of the "fat image" of herself in her subconscious mind.

She learned that it takes a minimum of 21 days to change a simple habit. Therefore, she knew that to change her tastes in food, her food habits would require just that—a minimum of 21 days.

She set her long-range goal as a 65-pound loss in six months, or earlier. Within this six-month period she set a short-range goal, the loss of 5 or possibly 10 pounds within the first 10 days. This would give her the psychological boost she needed to encourage her for the medium and long-range goals. Her medium goal was set for three months from the starting time—half way toward the long-range goal.

She reached her target of 65 pounds weight-loss a few days before the six months were over! And during that time her eating habits had been permanently changed. The habit of eating low-calorie, nutritious food was firmly established in her subconscious mind; she would never again enjoy fattening foods! She discovered that her subconscious mind worked exactly as programed. She no longer enjoyed doughnuts, french fries, or lemon custard pie.

In *exact sequence*, you erase the "fat" image in your mind by replacing it with a "thin" image, and then attain your long-sought goal of an *ideal body image!* You will be able to maintain it the rest of your life.

Now you can eat what you wish!

Surprisingly, we have repeatedly found in our classes that once the subconscious programing has been completed, you can eat whatever you wish! You can even go to parties and perhaps overeat for a day, but the next day your mind says to you in effect, "All right, you've had your fun, now don't eat for a day or two!" So you have no appetite for a day or two, and your excess calories are compensated for. You use no will power; it takes no effort whatsoever. This is how your subconscious mind works once it has been properly programed.

How to reprogram your subconscious

The next question quite naturally is, "Exactly how do I go about reprograming my subconscious mind?"

The first step is to have the desire to lose weight and to achieve an ideal body image. You have this desire already, or you would not be reading this book!

The next step is to set your goal weight. This *must* be *your* goal—not your spouse's goal, or your children's goal. It must be *your goal only!* At the end of this chapter is a goal chart where you can write down the number of pounds you want to lose, and set a short-range, medium-range, and long-range goal for your weight loss. There is also a space to insert a picture of you as you have looked in the past when you were the exact weight you now want to be. If you do not have such a picture, you can do something that may sound silly, but it works: look through a magazine until you find a picture of someone with the exact body image that is your goal, cut out and paste a picture of your face over the magazine picture. The reason this picture is so important is that it will stimulate your creative imagination. You can then use your mental imagery to picture yourself as you wish to look!

I remember a young woman who was successful in using this "magazine picture" method. Her's was an interesting story. She told us that she had actually had "reverse" subconscious programing. In early years she had been a very thin little girl. Her parents had always tried to persuade her to eat more in order to gain weight. However, no matter how much she ate, she did not gain the desired weight.

It was discovered while she was still very young that a simple health problem had been making it impossible for her to gain weight. When ·this health problem was corrected she proceeded to gain weight— at an alarming rate, because of her earlier programing and food habits. So, in reverse, her parents told her not to eat so much because she was now fat!

She stayed chubby until she began noticing boys. She knew they would not notice her unless she had a good figure. So, using the "magazine picture" method and visualizing herself with an ideal body image, she achieved her goal in approximately three months, and became an unusually beautiful person.

"Mental dieting" and your "slim image"

Remember, your mind thinks in pictures, and will always fashion your physical body exactly like the image you have of yourself in your subconscious mind. In our program of mental dieting, you will erase the "fat image" and reprogram a "slim image"!

The moment this "slim image" is firmly established in your subconscious mind, your physical body will gradually begin to look like the "thin image." This is one of the characteristics of the subconscious mind: it will bring into physical reality the mind images or pictures that have been programed.

All this will be done without any effort on your part! There is a secret here, however, and the secret is that you *must* see yourself as you would like to look—and *not* see yourself dieting or exercising on your way to your weight goal. Always, you must see *the end result*, not the methods used to get there. See yourself in your mind's eye as you want to look three or six months from the time you start. Try to "preconstruct" the feeling of how proud you will feel; imagine what a sense of accomplishment you will have! Everyone will admire you and ask you what you've done to make yourself look so marvelous! It is important to actually generate feeling, emotional reaction.

Keep your goal a secret

At this point, I must caution you not to tell anyone of what you are doing until you have accomplished your goal. There are two reasons for this: (1)—when you talk about your weight goals to others, you disperse the energy that is necessary to achieve them; and, (2)—when you tell others of your weight goals, particularly the people who have no knowledge of the power of the mind, they will naturally doubt. When they doubt, you doubt—and the program will not be successful.

One student was so excited when she started the mental diet class that she told her best friend about it. Her friend was very interested and wanted to know all about it. Then she told her two other friends, both of whom knew nothing about the power of the subconscious mind. They both questioned the idea of programing the subconscious mind. Because the student did not have enough knowledge as yet to counteract their doubts, their reactions set up a chain of doubts in her own mind and dispersed the energy she had generated when she was so excited about the method. She did not complete the first class.

Fortunately, she came to the next one and did not tell anyone of her program—until she had successfully lost 25 pounds! Do not tell anyone, or even talk of the reprograming of your subconscious mind in order to lose weight, until you have reached your weight goal. If anyone remarks that you seem to be losing weight, just pass over it and say something like, "Yes, and I'm not even trying!" So remember, keep your *weight goals a secret until you have achieved your ideal body image.* Then you can tell everyone exactly how you did it!

My three-step goal for weight loss:

I, <u>ANN Watson</u>, now weigh <u>140</u> lbs.
      (your name)

By <u>30 Sejst</u>, I will weigh <u>136</u> lbs.
    (short-range goal date)

By <u>30 Oct 1</u>, I will weigh <u>132</u> lbs.
   (half-way or medium-range
      goal date)   = Sept 3-92

My ideal body image

weight on <u>Nov 30</u>, is <u>130</u> lbs. or less
      (long-range goal date)

My ideal body image:

(Put your ideal body image picture here.)

'For the rest of your life
    you can have the ideal body
you have always wanted. . .''

Chapter 5

Beginning
Your Subconscious
Programing

You now know more about how your mind works and that you alone have the power to release yourself from the "prison of your mind." You are the only one who can consciously make the decision to do so. You probably have made that decision, because you are reading this book. Here you have found a way to do it, but now you must practice. Theories are fine, but action always does the work. So let us begin your subconscious programing which will obtain for you your ideal body image—for the rest of your life!

*The "mirror technique"
   with "words of power"*

The method, in two parts, will be described in detail. The first part is called the "mirror technique," and is used to eliminate three-fourths of your early negative programing. The second part is to use an affirmation—or "words of power." This second part helps you to understand the power of all the words you use every day.

The mirror technique is simple and is used primarily to raise your self-image. Your self-image is the picture you have of yourself—the inward picture of yourself, not the picture you present to the world through your personality.

The inward, private, secret picture you have of yourself is often quite different from the picture you present to others. Let me mention a student who was a good illustration of this truth. She presented to the world a picture of a brash, loud, bold woman, afraid of nothing, willing to take on any challenge. Inwardly, however, the picture was quite different. She was, in reality, a timid, frightened person. The picture of a person afraid of no one, ready to take any challenge, was her defense against the "hard, cruel world." After working with the mirror technique for a while, and improving her self-image, she was able actually to admit that her entire outward personality was a façade. At this very point of recognition and admission she began to become quieter and much more refined. Her true personality was released—she was a new, lovely, charming person.

What's more, after she had worked with her self-image, and had come to realize that her bold exterior was only an outward defense, she was able to lose weight! She finally realized that she had maintained her weight itself as a defense against the world.

*How others "programed" you
    for weight problems*

Your self-image was not formed exclusively by you. It became molded around the age of three by everyone who happened to be around you up to that time. It could have been your parents, brothers, sisters, aunts, uncles, grandparents, teachers, or friends.

Up to age three, children tend to accept all situations and statements at face value. This is because they do not have the critical faculty mentioned in Chapter 1, that enables them to "screen out" things they do not wish to accept. Thus they are programed with many negative statements and situations over which they have no control.

They do not even have the knowledge that the statements are negative. For example, if your mother was very fearful of all dogs, and conveyed that fear to you; then, even though you had never had a bad experience with a dog, you also would tend to be afraid of dogs. As a young child of limited knowledge, you would naturally look to your mother as having all knowledge and would believe her fear that all dogs are dangerous. In this way, you would have lost some of the "courage" you had at birth.

All babies are born almost fearless and with the potential for a perfect self-image, but by the time they are adults the self-image has been greatly distorted through experiences such as the example just cited. Every time you made a simple mistake—such as dropping and breaking a vase, and someone told you that you were a "bad girl" or a "bad boy," you accepted this statement as a "truth." You believed literally that you were bad from the top of your head to the tips of your toes. You felt that way—and your self-image was warped just a bit more. If someone had gently explained to you ways in which you could be a little more careful, your self-image would not have been affected. However, with most persons the damage has been inflicted time after time, until their self-image—far from being perfect—is very low indeed.

No one to blame

Your negative programing is not personal, it is highly impersonal. When others so acted as to "condition" your mind, there was no intent to harm you, there was just lack of knowledge. Only your emotions seem now to make it personal. If you can see through your emotions and recognize the negative programing for what it is, an impersonal condition, then it is fairly simple to reach through the negativity to the potential image of perfection that was present when you were born, and that you still have hidden in the deep recesses of your mind.

Remember that obesity is an appearance, a false image that you have accepted in your mind as a "truth" through your experiences as a child. You have only to realize that you are dealing with this false image (even though it may seem very real to you at the moment), not with your "real self" which has the potential of perfection.

If you now have a "fat" image in your mind, you can readily see that unless you can take the first steps toward improving your self-image—believe that you are worthy of achieving an ideal body image—you will not even bother to begin your subconscious programing.

This is why the mirror technique is so important—because it begins at once to raise your self-image. It is not necessary that you achieve a perfect self-image. If you can only make significant improvement you can become the type of person who can walk into a room full of strangers and make people turn to look at you and wonder who you are! A person with even a "half-perfect" self-image is so rare as to be immediately noticed.

Most people have suffered from negative programing with statements such as, "Come on, stupid, we'll be late." If you are called "stupid" enough times, eventually you will believe that you are stupid—even though it may have been said in a friendly manner. A father may in a loving, teasing way, say to his boy, "Hurry up and get in the car, stupid"—and give him a bear hug to show his love. The boy will tend to believe in his father, who obviously loves him and has never done him harm. So the boy must naturally assume that he really is stupid. After all, that's what his loving father thinks—so his subconscious mind tells him. Or, if you were a cute, chubby baby, perhaps your parents or grandparents called you "fatty" in a loving way. They loved you dearly, so because they called you "fatty," it must be true. Thus does the childish mind internalize and believe everything.

Can you see the importance of the very first steps in this program? An affirmation of the good things about yourself. If you can do this, the rest of the steps *will work*. This is the groundwork on which the program is built.

Not necessary to believe

It is *not necessary* for you to believe any of the statements or "words of power" you make to yourself. In fact, at first you will not believe any of them. You did not believe it the first time you were called "stupid" as a child, either. But, said many times, it was eventually believed. So, in essence, you are utilizing the same process—making to yourself this time a statement that you may not believe. But in time *you will believe it*, just as you believed the negative statements about you as a child.

Using the "mirror technique"

So now, let us get on with the "mirror technique" of raising your self-image. The first thing you must do upon awaking in the morning is to go to your mirror. Look yourself straight in the eye and say these "words of power": *"I like myself unconditionally!"*

Say this aloud if possible and with as much emotion as you can muster. At first, this will not be easy because your subconscious mind will talk back and say something like, "Who do you think you are kidding?" But pay no attention. Remember, at this point your mind is programed very negatively and you cannot believe this statement. Reminders will come to mind; such as, "I'd like myself if I weighed 25 pounds less."

Remember that at this point such thoughts are natural. Do not pay any attention to them; just keep on using the "mirror technique." It is an effective way to start the reprograming of your negative subconscious mind: making this affirmation—even without believing it!

The key word in this affirmation is *unconditionally*—not "if only this or that"—but, "I like myself *unconditionally*."

This statement is to be made the first thing upon awaking each morning and the last thing before going to bed at night. Go to your mirror, look yourself straight in the eyes, and say aloud with as much emotion as possible, *"I like myself unconditionally."* As many times as you can remember to do so during the day, repeat this affirmation, even if you are not able to use a mirror. The more times you can remember to say it each day, the sooner you will raise your self-image.

A 21-day program

This must be done for 21 consecutive days. If you miss for even one day, begin your 21 days over again—remember, the minimum time required to change a habit. After all, this is what you are doing: changing a negative habit into a positive one.

Some of my students have invented clever ways of helping themselves to remember to keep making the affirmation. One wrote in lipstick on her bathroom mirror, "*I like myself unconditionally.*" She also put 21 "X's" on her mirror. Each evening after saying her last affirmation, she erased one of the "X's;" thereby enabling herself to keep track of the 21 days.

Another student used the "cue card" approach. She wrote these "words of power" on three 3" x 5" cards, putting one in her desk at work, one on the dashboard of her car, and one on her desk calendar at home. She was thus reminded to say the words, "*I like myself unconditionally,*" often during the day.

This simple statement will often save your day. If you encounter an unpleasant experience, such as your boss scolding you for something that is not your fault, get out your card when you are alone, and say to yourself, *"I like myself unconditionally."* (On the job it may not be possible—or prudent—to say it aloud!) But said even to yourself it will begin to generate positive feelings to offset the negative feelings generated by your boss.

One student, utilizing the "cue card" idea, put one of his cards on the inside of the door of his refrigerator. In his usual nightly foraging for food, he would see the card, and say this statement aloud. To his surprise, he found that this affirmation helped him to curb the craving for food. Because his craving was caused by a feeling of not being loved, he had been substituting food for love. Thus the affirmation got to the cause of the problem. It gradually neutralized his feeling of not being loved; and the craving for food gradually subsided. Thus, as his self-image was raised by just this simple statement, he came to realize that he was worthy of having an ideal body image. For the first time in his life he was able to stick to a diet; and, consequently, lost a great deal of weight in a short time.

Another student found the best time to make the affirmation was when she was driving to work. At home it was not possible for her to say it aloud, although she did look into her mirror and say it to herself. But going to and from work, alone in her car, she was able actually to shout out the words, *"I like myself unconditionally!"* She said she found that after a difficult day at work, the affirmation helped her to regain her sense of well-being; and, by the time she arrived at home she was in a good mood.

Certainly she and her family benefited by this very simple aid in her reprograming of her subconscious mind!

When you first begin using the mirror technique, you may have one of several reactions. You may laugh, feel very uncomfortable, or you may even cry. Don't be concerned about any of these reactions. They are all natural, and every student has experienced one or more of them—with the exception of a very few who already liked themselves.

The important thing is to keep saying the affirmation for 21 consecutive days. This cannot be overemphasized. It *must* be for *21 consecutive days*. If you miss even one day, you *must* begin your 21 days over again. Even the simplest habit takes 21 days to become a habit; or, in other words, to be programed into your subconscious mind.

Affirmation a lifetime help

Now this does not mean that after 21 days you should stop making the affirmation. Keep on saying it because even after you have realized your ideal body image this statement will do amazing, seemingly miraculous, things for you. As time goes on, you will find that it will help to open a door to the creative level of your mind. Your creativity has been there all the time, but in your negative childhood programing, the door to this creativity was slammed shut and firmly locked. The simple affirmation, *"I like myself unconditionally,"* will help to unlock that door. You may be surprised to find yourself doing things you have only dreamed of—painting, writing, even starting a new business. Nothing is impossible when you open the door to the creative level of your mind.

We are bombarded every day with negative things—through television, radio, newspapers, and other media. It is necessary to neutralize as much of this negativity as possible through positive state- ments, words, and even songs—anything that puts you in a positive frame of mind. Do not accept any more negative programing! You are in control of your own mind and you are also aware of the damage the negative programing will do. Do not allow it from this day on! You are the master of your mind. You can decide if you are going to allow a person or sit- uation to control you—or if you are going to control yourself.

Suppose you arrive at your job in the morning feeling just great. Your coworker comes in bleary- eyed from a sleepless night and his first words to you are, "What a rotten day this is going to be." Are you going to agree with him and thus allow your coworker's statement to program your mind for a rot- ten day? Or are you going to say, "I feel just great and it's going to be a great day for me." At that point you have a choice, don't you? Will you agree just to be polite, or do you make your own great day? It is al- ways up to you.

Are you beginning to get the picture? You are the

master of every situation as far as your attitudes are concerned. The result is in your *reaction* to any situation and in your *attitude* toward it. Even the worst situation can be made better by your reaction to it if you try to see the good.

Deal with the facts

There is a simple method you can use to analyze situations that bother you. Put down on paper the facts—not your opinion, just the facts. Nine times out of ten you will discover that facts will be quite simple and innocent and that your opinions about the facts are the negative factors.

So it is with your weight problem. The simple fact may be that you got that way by consuming too many calories. That is the fact. Your opinion is that you will never be able to lose all those pounds, that even if you try you don't have the necessary will power, that you will really have to suffer if you go on a diet, etc. Do not add your opinion to the simple facts. Just work on the facts.

Thus, with the beginning step—using the "mirror technique" with the positive "words of power"—you will get rid of your uncertainties, your fears, your worries, your untrue opinions; all the things that up to this time have kept you from ever trying to reach your ideal body weight.

Begin to use this effective technique. Go to your mirror, look yourself right in the eyes, and say aloud with as much emotion and conviction you can muster, *"I like myself unconditionally!"*

Chapter 6

How Important
Is Relaxation?

"What is relaxation?" For our purposes here, we could define relaxation as a technique or skill for attaining greater control of our bodies and emotions.

It is important to learn how to relax because we live in a society that constantly produces tension, and tension—or stress—contributes to the development of such problems as heart attacks, ulcers, or colitis. More important to you in solving a weight problem is the discovery that stress is a major contributor to obesity. When a person is under stress, the adrenal cortex produces more cortisone and that in itself may tend to cause an "inflated" look. Moreover, because of stress many people develop a pattern of "ritual eating" that leads to obesity.

If undue stress is inherent in your job and you cannot eliminate it, get a less stressful job. You will live longer. Being under great stress most of the time will, of course, do more than make you overweight. It provides a quick route to an early death.

Stress, obesity, and survival

Extensive research was conducted with rats exposed to stressful situations. One group of rats was subjected to kinds of stress similar to that which human beings face every day—too much heat, cold, frustration, hunger, fatigue, and unpleasant situations. Another group of rats had a lovely life with plenty of food, rest, and recreation. Autopsies were performed on both groups. In the stress group, adrenal and thymus glands, and stomach linings were suffused with blood, misshapen, and enlarged with disease. In the other group these organs were smooth and healthy. The changes in the organs of the stress rats were caused by the emotions involved in stress. Similar things happen to us when we are exposed to prolonged stress—unless we do something to control it.

One of my students told the class that when he was employed in an executive position, he had been subjected to just the kind of stress we are talking about here. His supervisors put on a great deal of pressure to get more accounts, and he had several employees to manage. He did not know how to cope with stress and, eventually, had a heart attack. His doctor told him that if he didn't learn to relax—and also to shed his excess weight—he would be jeopardizing his life.

Here we see one of the reasons so many men in our society have heart attacks and die long before their wives do. The student just mentioned had been reared to always "put on a front." As a little boy he had been discouraged from crying or showing any emotion—because this was not "manly." Therefore, on the surface, he seemed to be very even-tempered; but, at times, he was raging inside.

Even when he suffered pain, he endured it with great stoicism, just as many such persons do, sometimes even in extreme cases. His friends and physicians had wondered at his amazing "tranquility" in unusually trying circumstances. But, of course, he had been so programed that showing a reaction to pain was "unmanly."

His mental programing—never to show emotions—was also directly tied to his weight problem. He used food in a subconscious attempt to get rid of anger, hostility, and the guilt feelings he could not allow himself to express outwardly.

When he learned how to relax; and, finally, to realize that it was acceptable to show his true feelings, the excess weight was shed without further difficulty.

We all find ourselves in stressful situations every day. The alarm goes off late, we miss a bus, the mortgage comes due, the paycheck is late, we overwork and become tired—all such situations contribute to a continuing condition of stress.

Ritual eating

How do we cope with stress? Ritual eating, as we mentioned earlier, is one of the ways and we find this response pattern in many obese persons. Ritual eating may be defined as "compulsive or unconscious eating." It is an attempt to subconsciously get rid of tension, fear, or anxiety.

Persons who have developed this habit rarely are aware of what they eat or even how it tastes. They just shovel it in. They eat too quickly for their taste buds to send the message of taste to their brains, so they rarely have any taste enjoyment in eating. Like some other habits, eating for these people fills an emotional need. As an alcoholic rushes for a drink, a smoker reaches for a cigarette, these people turn to food.

Let me tell you about a student whose husband spent many nights working late. She resented being married but not "having a husband." As a kind of compensation she would often buy a very large pie heaped with mounds of whipped cream and eat the whole thing. She said she does not remember how it tasted, but when she finished the pie, she had a "So there!" feeling of revenge against frustrations.

Another student, a plump young girl, with a very pretty face, finally recognized while in class that she had been deliberately eating two helpings of cake for dessert because of her suppressed anger at her mother.

This may sound like a childish reaction—to harm yourself in order to get even with someone; yet, many people do just that because they are not aware of their emotional hang-ups.

To become aware that you have a tendency to overeat in a stressful situation is the first step toward breaking the habit. Once again, that is simply what it is, a habit that can be reprogramed in your subconscious mind. If you become aware that you have feelings of repressed rage, hostility, or frustration, there is a simple way to get rid of them. For example, any physical activity before meals will help you to get rid of excess adrenalin in your body. You see, at any time you are acting under stress, you generate too much adrenalin and if you do not get rid of it, it will in time break down the weakest parts of your body. So, smash a tennis ball against a wall, punch a punching bag, wash down your walls, run around the block. Any physical activity appropriate to your physical condition will help you to "work off" the excess adrenalin.

Another reason, the most important reason, you must learn to relax is simply that it is the *only* way to reach your subconscious mind. Reach it you must in order to reprogram it and replace all the negativity lodged there with positive attitudes.

Many people are totally unaware that they are tense—and perhaps have been all their lives. These people think everyone feels the same way they do. They do not have any basis for knowing the difference between tension and relaxation. Thus, it is important to make a brain cell impression, or imprint, so that the difference in feeling between tension and relaxation can be discerned.

Learning relaxation

Here is an exercise to demonstrate tension, so that you can better recognize how the opposite—*relaxation* —feels.

1. Hold both arms straight out in front of you. Slowly close both fists very tightly. The muscular contraction you feel up to your shoulders is tension.

2. Direct your attention to your jaw, and clench your teeth; frown as hard as you can, then close your eyes as tightly as you can. This is tension!

Remember: tension is muscular contraction; relaxation is muscular rest, "limpness." Relaxation is a sensation you must get the "feel" of in order to recognize it.

A relaxation exercise

In the following relaxation exercise, try to get this "feel" for relaxation so that you will have a positive brain cell impression that will help you to be aware of the difference between tension and relaxation.

Sit down in your favorite chair with your feet flat on the floor. Put your hands loosely in your lap. Take three deep breaths to rid your system of excess carbon dioxide.

With the eyes open:

1. Tense both hands and arms. Pause. Now relax all tension, release all pressure, letting your muscles feel limp. (Do not "try hard" to make this happen, just "let" it happen.) If you are able to relax only one finger the first time, that is fine. In this exercise, "practice makes perfect." You learn how to relax, just as you learned how to swim or how to drive a car, by practice.

2. Gently contract and tense the muscles of your forehead and around your eyes. Pause. Now relax all tension.

3. Now gently tense the muscles of your jaw and around your mouth. Pause. Now relax all tension, release all pressure.

4. Gently tense the muscles of your shoulders and your back. Pause. Now relax all tension, release all pressure, and place these areas of your body into a deep state of relaxation, going deeper and deeper every time you practice this exercise.

5. Now take a deep breath and feel your chest relax as you exhale.

6. Gently tense the abdominal muscles. Pause. Relax all tension, release all pressures.

7. Now, using your creative imagination, relax the chest and stomach internally. Pause. Relax deeply.

8. Still using creative imagination, relax all of your organs internally; the glands, even the cells! "Allow" them to function in a normal, relaxed manner.

9. Tense your feet and toes. Pause. Now relax your feet and toes.

10. Now relax the entire body from the top of your head all the way down to the tips of your toes.
Now, using your creative imagination, "feel" a wave of relaxation, like a wave of the ocean, sweeping over you completely from the top of your head to the tips of your toes. As the wave sweeps over you, each muscle and nerve that is touched is now relaxing completely. Let this wave of relaxation once again sweep over you, relaxing you completely from the top of your head to the very tips of your toes.

Repeat the entire above exercise with your eyes closed.

If you have trouble relaxing, an easy way to get the "feel" of relaxation is for someone to read the above exercise to you. You will just listen and allow the sensation of relaxation to happen. Remember, do not use "active relaxation," which is the thought, "I'm going to relax even if it kills me." Use "passive relaxation." Let it happen. If just one hand, or just one leg, or even just a finger becomes truly relaxed the first time, that's progress. Remember, up to this time you may have been completely tense, from head to toes. Each time you practice this exercise, you will find that it is easier.

One student used a tape recorder to record a reading of this exercise. She played it to herself and in this way was able to get the "feel" of relaxation, and thereby make a brain cell "imprint" for relaxation. After you once get the feel of it, each exercise makes it easier to "replay" the feeling when ever you get into a tense sensation.

Another student also tried to use a tape recording, but did not like the sound of her voice. This was the reaction of some others, too, so the instructors of each class now make their own tapes, and this has proven to be successful. The time for learning the art of relaxation has been cut in half.

Relaxation opens the door to awareness

The relaxation exercise presented above should be practiced at least once, and preferably twice, each day until you really do develop a "feel" for it. Once you get this feeling of relaxation, you will have opened the door to reprogram your subconscious mind.

Remember that only with relaxation can you reach your subconscious mind.

It has been found that the best times to do these exercises are in the mid-afternoon for "morning persons," and in the mid-morning for "night people." If you are a person who loves to get up early in the morning and you are very energetic then, but run down by afternoon, you are a morning person. On the other hand, if you hate to get up early in the morning and love to stay up until all hours of the night, you are a night person. So decide which type you are, and do the relaxation exercise at the time best suited for you.

There are some vitally beneficial effects in this relaxation process besides the obvious ones of help in coping with your everyday problems and of reprograming your subconscious mind. It has been found in our classes that, during the relaxation exercise, images will float from your subconscious mind to your conscious mind that tell you exactly why you have a weight problem.

It was interesting for one student to find that her problem was directly in line with the guilt feelings she had because of never having been able to live up to her father's expectations. Her father's expectations had seemed unreasonable for a small girl to live up to, and she never felt that she could do so.

Outwardly, she seemed not to have a weight problem; she had, in fact, a beautiful, slim figure. However, she told the class that she had always had to fight the compulsion to eat rich foods and when she succumbed to temptation she had tremendous feelings of guilt. She was so very tired of having to use her will power to fight food temptations and guilt feelings that she was ready to give up and forget the whole thing. She was absolutely delighted when she discovered that it was not her battle at all, but in reality her father's battle. In her childish way, she had made it her own.

Another student, by way of contrast, discovered in a period of relaxation that he had taken on the entire burden of his mother's untimely death, when he was only a very young child. As children often do at that age, he assumed that he must have been a very bad boy for his mother to have died. It is sad but true that, unless children are helped to realize that they had nothing to do with a parent's death, they very often do have great feelings of guilt. Their whole lives may be spent in subconsciously trying to atone for it.

In the case just described, the student felt that he had no right to look good, that he must carry a burden of overweight the rest of his life. Remember, consciously he was totally unaware of this, but subconsciously his whole outlook on life was related to that one childhood tragedy. No one had perceived his guilt feelings in relation to this overwhelming experience or tried to help him to neutralize them.

You can now be responsible

Fortunately, most overweight problems do not stem from such traumatic experiences, but originate in simple negative programing performed in our childhood by someone who had no idea what he was doing to our minds. No one can be blamed for this, because until a few short years ago, no one knew much about how the mind functions. But now a great deal is known, and after you have finished reading this book, you will know how you can let your mind change yourself. You will then have no one to blame but yourself if you don't make necessary changes. Remember, if you change yourself, you also change the world around you.

Now you realize the great importance of relaxation. If you do not learn how to relax, you will never get to the root, or cause, of your problems. You will forever be treating the symptoms; and, unfortunately, this is not a lasting solution. The symptoms are always cropping up, just like a crop of weeds. The only way to get rid of the weeds is to pull them up by the roots.

Nature's own "tranquilizer"

So the only way to get rid of your weight problem permanently is to get to the cause of it and eliminate that cause. There just is no other way! <u>Your weight problem is the direct result of your thinking, triggered by an underlying emotional problem</u>.

Many people resort to alcohol, drugs, or other escape mechanisms to escape the effects of everyday stress and their emotional hang-ups. But you can dissolve the negative emotions and stresses in a very natural way: use nature's own tranquilizer—*relaxation!*

"Use the creative
    powers of your mind."

Chapter 7

Creative Imagination

What is creative imagination? It is a tool you can use to reprogram the subconscious mind. Your mind thinks only in pictures, so it is essential that your creative imagination be developed in order for you to more fully use the creative powers of your mind.

All children are born with impressive powers of creativity; but, unfortunately, through lack of understanding among adults as to how the mind functions, most children both at home and at school have been taught to disregard anything that comes from that creative function of the mind, the imagination. Children in most schools are taught to think rationally and reason problems out; but, unfortunately, this is only one mode of mind function. The other factor is creative imagination. Although a child may in early life use his creative imagination to some extent, by age 10 or 12 he has been taught to almost completely ignore this most important function. Thus, by the time he is an adult and does occasionally have a flash of creativity, the tendency is to disregard it as "pure imagination."

A creativity experiment

Try a little experiment at this point to see if your creative imagination is still functioning, even to a slight degree. Close your eyes and for a period of three to four minutes, try to visualize an apple—any color or kind of apple you wish.

By the picture that appears in your mind's eye, you can determine if you must work at reviving your creative imagination; or, if you were one of the fortunate ones who escaped the full effects of "social erasure" of creative imagination.

Did you see a full, red, delicious apple, or a green or a half-eaten apple? Perhaps an apple with a worm in it, or even a whole apple tree with many apples on it. It does not matter what you saw as long as you saw something. Some students say that they did not actually see a picture; they simply had a feeling or imagined they were seeing an apple. Even this is some proof that you have the faculty of creative imagination still active and working for you.

A statement from your subconscious

There is an interesting by-product of this mental exercise. The picture of the apple you saw is also a kind of statement from your subconscious mind telling you things about yourself. For instance, if you saw a half-eaten apple, your mind may be telling you that you have a feeling that someone is taking from you things you feel are yours. If you saw a worm in your apple, then you have a message telling you that you feel you are not perfect.

One girl saw several withered, wrinkled peaches in a bowl at her home. She said that these peaches were supposed to be eaten with her former diet, but she could not bring herself to eat them so they almost completely dried up. This seemed to tell her that she had a feeling of rebellion toward dieting. It was up to her to find out exactly why she felt that way. Later, in class during a relaxation period, she discovered the answer. She had a younger sister whom she felt always got her own way while she never did. Therefore, inwardly she always felt rebellious although outwardly she did not show it. When her doctor told her to go on a diet, she complied with her doctor's order—at first. Then, inwardly, the rebellion began and revealed itself in the three withered peaches in the bowl, part of her diet. She said this sudden flash of insight told her more about herself than she had ever known before, and it explained many things she did that were a puzzlement to herself as well as to her family.

In order to develop the creative faculty of your mind to its fullest, it does help to jog it into activity with pictures. So, as suggested in Chapter 4, get a picture of yourself as you would like to look; or, if you have no picture, get a magazine picture and put a cut-out picture of your own face over it. Put it where you can see it many times during the day, like the student who put it on his refrigerator. It was a picture taken when he was in the army. Of course, army life helps to turn flabby fat into solid muscle, and he had never looked or felt better! He said that every time he was tempted to go into the refrigerator for a snack, that picture reminded him of his desire to look like that picture once again! Then, before his relaxation exercise, he first took a good, long look at his picture, went into a deep relaxation with the image of himself as he wanted to look very fresh in his imagination.

The levels of your mind

An explanation of why this method works will be beneficial right here, because if you know why it works, you will be more likely to carry it out. In the case above, we can say that a brain-cell impression was imprinted within the "alpha level" of the mind simply by using creative imagination and passive relaxation. What is the "alpha level" of your mind?

You have four levels of activity in your mind:

Beta level (conscious mind). This is the "action" level of your mind and the one you are most aware of. You do your "surface" thinking and rationalizing at this level. Here you receive information from your environment through your senses of seeing, hearing, tasting, smelling, and feeling. You do only about 10 percent of your thinking at this level. Here, brain wave vibrations are at 28 cycles per second.

Alpha level (subconscious mind). This is the "creative" level of your mind and you can reach it *only* through relaxation. Within this level lies your inspiration, creativity, tranquility, extrasensory perception, memory, and other amazing powers! Relaxation cannot be emphasized enough because it is the *only* way to reach this level. Vibrations here are at a lower rate, between 7 and 14 cycles per second. There are several ways to recognize when you are at the alpha level. You may see a blue light in your "mind's eye"—or other various colors. Perhaps your forehead may feel as if you have a tight band around it. Another sensation may be a feeling of lightness or floating. But, whatever it is, you will have your own way of recognizing this level in your own mind. There are varied and different clues, but you must be alert and become aware of what your particular ones are.

Theta level. This level involves deeper levels of meditation and concentration. Zen masters, with years of study and experience, have been said to reach this spiritual level easily. Here vibrations are from 4 to 7 cycles per second.

Delta level. This level is associated with deep sleep or unconsciousness. Very little is known about this level, where vibrations are at the lowest rate, between one-half and four cycles.

So, you can see that in learning the relaxation methods we are discussing in this book, you are also learning how to slow your brain wave patterns from 28 cycles per second to around 7. At the same time you are projecting an image which is helping you to utilize the great creative level of your subconscious mind, thus allowing the creativity to "float" to the conscious mind.

The basic relaxation exercise

Here is an exercise to help you slow down your brain wave cycles to the alpha level and "tap" into this creative level—in order to program your ideal body image. Please read the complete exercise before beginning it, and then follow the exact sequence.

To enter the alpha level of awareness, assume a comfortable position, arms and legs uncrossed, hands resting comfortably in your lap.

Close your eyes, take a deep breath and, while exhaling, mentally repeat the word *"relax"* several times.

To enter a still deeper level of alpha consciousness,

take another deep breath and mentally repeat the words *"relax within"* several times.

To enable you to enter an even deeper, more extended level of alpha consciousness, you will relax all areas of your body—beginning at your head and scalp.

As you relax down through each area, you will reach a deeper, more extended level of alpha consciousness and slow your brain wave cycles to about eight cycles per second. You may picture this, if you wish, in order to help you to more quickly slow down the cycles. Picture wheels revolving very fast at first, then gradually slowing down—as you are relaxing from the top of your head down to the very tips of your toes. As the wheels revolve more and more slowly, you are feeling more and more peaceful and relaxed.

With your creative imagination, relax your scalp and the top of your head. Imagine relaxing your forehead and face muscles. Allow your teeth to separate slightly. Allow this sensation of relaxation to flow slowly downward throughout the body, all the way down to your toes.

Now imagine relaxing your neck and shoulders, relax your arms and hands. Imagine this relaxation slowly flowing downward. The "wheels" are beginning to slow down and are now turning more and more slowly.

Now, imagine relaxing your back muscles, your chest muscles and your abdominal muscles; imagine this relaxation flowing downward, all the way down to your toes.

Imagine now, relaxing down through your hips and legs, through the calves and feet, all the way down to your toes.

It is a pleasant feeling to be so deeply relaxed.

You are now in a deeper, more extended level of alpha consciousness. The wheels are turning very, very slowly now.

To enter a deeper, still more extended level, imagine yourself in a serene, relaxing setting, your perfect place of relaxation, wherever that may be. It may be on a beautiful sandy beach, under the pines in the mountains, beside a peaceful river, or even in your own home. Wherever your ideal place of relaxation may be, imagine yourself there now. Spend about five minutes at that place and allow yourself to relax even more completely. Take a deep breath and enter an even deeper level, with the wheels revolving ever so slowly.

As you are in this dreamlike state, imagine yourself standing on the bank of a slowly moving river. There is a small boat waiting for you. You enter the boat; and, resting lazily on pillows in the bottom of the boat, you set the boat adrift on that lazy river. The boat is rocking gently from the motion of the water, back and forth, rising and falling, rocking gently as the boat just drifts on and on. As the boat drifts down and down on the river, you feel only the gentle rocking, listening to the lapping of the water against the boat, smelling a pleasant fragrance of dampness and then becoming aware of the warm sunlight. Floating lazily downstream, feeling the warm sunlight and the caressing of the soft breeze as it passes over you, you drift gently on and on. Along the river bank, the birds are singing a happy song, insects chirping and humming—such a beautiful, lazy summer day.

Now there comes to your awareness delightful, fragrant scents of the flowers growing along the river bank, and the freshly cut grass in the fields, where mowers are still working. As you drift lazily by, one of the mowers waves at you in a cheery greeting.

You have a feeling of great contentment, serenity, and total peace as you drift drowsily down and down the river, with the gentle rocking of the boat. Just let yourself feel it all for a few moments. Be totally aware of your surroundings, the songs of the birds and the insects chirping. The fragrance of the flowers and the freshly cut grass.

As you continue to drift slowly down the river, drifting and drifting with the warm sunlight shining on you, you are completely and totally relaxed with a feeling of great peace. You are in touch with the deep center of your being, that center within all of us that is never disturbed by outer conditions, that creative center that can be reached only by deep relaxation.

Assume your ideal body image

Now the boat bumps gently against the grasses along the bank, the grasses slow it down, and finally it stops. Very slowly you climb out of the boat; and, as you look up, you see standing before you an image of your own body. Not as your body is now, but your body as you would like it to be and as it has the possibility of being. This image of your body does not surprise you, or startle you in any way. You have a "knowingness" inside of you that accepts this image as a reality. Now this image is becoming clearer and clearer to you, and more and more real. You are now seeing it very clearly and seeing it in its full size and dimension. The proportion and symmetry of this body is exactly as you wish it to be.

Now step forward and into that body and feel yourself in that body so you can try it out and make certain it is just the body you wish to have. If there is a change you wish to make, let that change take place now.

Move around in that body, feel its strength and agility, the ease of movement. Feel its dynamic aliveness, its surging vitality and make certain that its appearance is what you really desire. As you feel yourself in that body, coming to know that body, knowing that it really is your body, your present physical body is merging into that new mold. You are now, at this moment, moving toward the realization of your ideal body image, and henceforth will be doing whatever is needed to achieve that body as quickly as possible.

It may be a matter of exercise, of eating less, of better nutrition, better environment. Whatever it is, you will do it, allowing nothing to stand in your way as you go about creating the conditions most favorable to quickly achieving that ideal body.

From now on, that model will exist in your subconscious mind at the alpha level; it will be there constantly. It will be a magnetic, attracting force, a vital force that will draw and compel you to do what is necessary until your present physical body and the image you have of your ideal body are merged as one.

Now, using your creative imagination, visualize yourself doing all of those things necessary for obtaining your ideal body image as soon as possible. You see yourself sitting down at mealtime, eating only low-calorie, nutritious food, eating slowly, and feeling satisfied with a small portion of food.

You see yourself saying no to high-calorie foods that have been your temptation in the past.

Now, see yourself in a full-length mirror, turning this way and turning that way. You are very pleased with the way you look. You feel a surge of joy, knowing that you have achieved your perfect body concept.

But for now, put that ideal body image out of your consciousness, let it fade from your awareness—it will remain vivid and effective in your subconscious mind.

Say now the master affirmation, *"I like myself unconditionally,"* three times.

Terminating the exercise

Now, to come out of the alpha level, slowly stretch your arms over your head, flex your muscles and you will be out of the alpha level and in the beta level of you mind.

This is it

This mental exercise should be practiced once a day as soon as you have learned to relax effectively. This *is* the reprograming of your subconscious mind. This is how to do it. As you slow down your brain wave cycles and see your ideal body image, you are making a pattern in your brain cells. When that pattern is clearly etched, your physical body must *become* that pattern. Your physical body follows the dictates of the subconscious mind.

No more will power needed

When this programing is complete and the pattern is vivid in your brain cells, you will not have to use will power to control your eating habits; your subconscious mind will take this over for you and do it much more effectively than you have ever been able to do it consciously. This is the same subconscious mind that regulates the digestion of your food, the beating of your heart, makes you take a breath at the right time. Your subconscious mind can do all this without any conscious interference from you, and it does it much better than you could by thinking about it.

There are a few ways to tell if your subconscious programing is complete: if you do not desire any of the things that formerly tempted you; or if your appetite has subsided; or if high-calorie foods do not appeal to you as much as they formerly did.

The secret of "mental dieting"

The success of this subconscious programing is determined by one little fact, one secret, that most people are unaware of. The secret is that your subconscious mind does not know the difference between a real or an imagined experience. So, if you imagine yourself standing on a scale and you see that scale in your mind's eye as showing your weight to be 125 pounds—if you do this enough times for the "experience" to be etched in your brain cells, your subconscious mind will soon see to it that you do weigh 125 pounds. It takes orders from these pictures in your mind, and it must bring that picture into being.

You can now see why you are having weight problems. At this moment there is an image of yourself in your mind as being overweight, and because your subconscious must bring into reality what it "sees," you are just that way—fat! Your subconscious mind must do this because its function is to make real that which is pictured in your mind.

However, as you do these mental exercises, you will soon change the "fat" image you now have in your subconscious mind to a "slim" image. When that happens, you will have your ideal body image. It's as simple as that!

So now, turn the page and reflect on "My Daily Pledge," a pledge to yourself to utilize every day the power of creative imagination. This creative power will help you to achieve the goals that make you the person you want to be.

My daily pledge:

"Each day I will use mental imagery.

"1. As I deeply relax, I visualize the image of the body I want to have, and hold that image for *six seconds.*

"2. I will also say the affirmation: *I am now the exact weight for my particular body and bone structure, and I look and feel marvelous!*"

Chapter 8

Forgiveness

There is yet more that must be done in order to lose weight and keep it off: forgive anyone against whom you hold any resentment.

What does forgiveness have to do with losing weight?

Research has shown that feelings of resentment, condemnation of others, remorse, or hostility are at the root of a host of psychosomatic ills—including obesity.

Have you ever heard someone say, "I can forgive but I can't forget"? It is impossible to really forgive without forgetting. The forgetting is one of the elements of forgiving. Forgiveness is clearing the mind of negativity. It is releasing a negative emotion, and in releasing it, also releasing the excess weight you are holding on to.

There are many reasons people cannot "let go" of weight. Research has shown that the weight syndrome is much more complex than had previously been thought. It all begins in the mind; it is absolutely necessary to dissolve the negative emotions.

We punish ourselves

When we subconsciously harbor resentment against another person, guilt feelings that consciously we are not aware of may lead us to punish ourselves in various ways—including getting fat! In this way we feel we have atoned for our negative feeling toward the other person. Almost all my students have found it necessary to forgive one or more persons. (The only student that did not have anyone else to forgive, had to forgive herself.)

Forgiving one's self and others is a necessary step in this process of letting go our excess weight. Everyone has something--or someone—who has "done him wrong," and he may hold a grudge against that person. It is important to let the grudge be neutralized.

Forgiveness is a practical, everyday principle of health and progress. As an added bonus, it will stabilize your weight. Even though you feel someone has harmed you, nothing is gained by continuing a feeling of ill will toward the other person. You may not want to associate with that person and indeed you need not do so. But it is imperative that you release the feeling of ill will toward him. This person may not even be aware that you have a grudge against him, so it is not harming him. But it is doing you a great deal of harm, mentally and physically. It has been shown that grudges and hatred toward anyone have actually caused many illnesses such as cancer, heart attacks, colitis, etc., besides the more common weight problem.

Forgive others; forgive yourself

It is imperative that you also forgive yourself. If you have harmed someone and he forgives you, he is released. He is free. Forgiveness is a mental release on his part, but if you cannot forgive yourself and you continue to carry a sense of guilt, you are not released even though the other person may long ago have forgiven you. Unless you also forgive yourself, you will continue to suffer.

For many people, this is part of their weight syndrome. They cannot release or forgive themselves or other people. As long as they continue to hold on to these negative feelings, they will also hold on to their weight.

A student told us that he thought he had harmed a friend and he was unhappy and ashamed. He said he thought his friend was avoiding him; and, because of his burden of guilt, he also avoided his friend. After the class discussion on forgiveness, he went to his friend to apologize; and, to his surprise, his friend said, "Why, I don't know of any wrong you have done to me. I did think you had been avoiding me, but I couldn't figure out why." From this experience the student realized that there had been no sense of disharmony on his friend's part. The problem was entirely in his own mind.

Even though someone may have wronged you and you did nothing to deserve it, you still should not hold on to a grudge. "Righteous" indignation is just as harmful as any other kind. It is still a negative emotion, righteous or not. All it does is harm you.

A "miracle" in forgiveness

This principle was dramatically illustrated in the experience of one of my students. She was an intelligent woman of genuine professional accomplishment. Her husband had left her and married a much younger woman. There seemed to be ample reason for her to believe that she had been the injured party. This had all happened several years previously, but she had never forgiven the man; and, indeed, it would have been a difficult thing to do.

Her ex-husband seemed well-to-do, happily married to the other woman and she seemed to be left holding the bag. Her mind was full of bitterness—and her body was very much overweight. It was almost as if because her husband had chosen another woman over her, that she had tried to make herself as unattractive as possible. Eating was also an emotional outlet for her; it filled the void of not feeling loved. As long as she held on to all her negative feelings, she was not able to release her weight.

Finally, it got through to her that it would be impossible for her to lose weight until she first let go of the grudge against her ex-husband. She was still tied to him with ties of bitterness and resentment. She worked very hard with the "forgiveness" principle. At last, she was able to fully forgive him. Almost at once several very interesting things began to happen. The first was that she began to lose weight because her neurotic desire for food was gone. She began to like herself again through saying the master affirmation (Chapter 5). She began to feel much better and to look much better.

Not too long afterward, her ex-husband took the initiative in coming to see her to make right some things in which he felt he had been unfair with her. A miracle? No, she had just let go of her resentment. She had been able to forgive the person she had considered her enemy.

If you have ever been in a situation similar to this one, remember this simple test: if you still remember the hurt, you have not forgiven. You must forget in order to forgive. And forgive you must! For your own sake, alone.

You will now do a mental exercise to help you in forgiving the person or persons against whom you hold any ill feelings. If you have no one in mind, you may find it necessary to forgive yourself. So give it some thought now. Who is it that you still have negative feelings toward, no matter how slight?

You will use your creative imagination; and, again, use the words of power.

A mental exercise for forgiveness

You are seated comfortably in your favorite chair, your feet flat on the floor. Your hands rest easily on your lap. Take three deep breaths, deep to the bottom of your lungs, slowly exhaling each time. Close your eyes.

1. Tense both hands and arms. Pause. Now relax all tension. Release all pressure, letting your muscles feel limp.

2. Gently contract and tense the muscles of your forehead and around your eyes. Pause. Now relax all tension. Let your muscles become limp; release all pressures.

3. Now gently tense the muscles of your jaw and around your mouth. Pause. Now relax all tension; release all pressures.

4. Gently tense the muscles of your shoulders and back. Pause. Now relax all tension; release all pressures, and place these areas of your body into a deep state of relaxation, going deeper every time you practice this exercise.

5. Now take a deep breath and feel your chest relax as you exhale.

6. Gently tense the abdominal muscles. Pause. Relax all tension; release all pressures.

7. Now, using your creative imagination, relax the chest and abdominal muscles internally. Pause. Relax deeply.

8. With your mind, "relax" all of your organs internally; your glands, and even your cells, and "allow" them to function in a normal, relaxed manner.

9. Tense your feet and toes. Pause. Now relax your feet and toes.

10. Now relax the entire body from the top of your head all the way down to the tips of your toes.

Using the creative imagination, imagine a wave of relaxation, like a wave of the ocean, sweeping over you completely from the top of your head to the very tips of your toes. As the wave sweeps over you, each muscle and nerve it touches is relaxed completely. Now, search out any remaining tense areas and let them relax completely. Let this wave of relaxation once again sweep over you, relaxing you completely from the top of your head to the very tips of your toes.

Now, as you are in a complete state of physical and mental relaxation—using your creative imagination—imagine that you are sitting in a motion picture theatre. The beautiful, red velvet curtains begin to open. They slide noiselessly to each side and you see a large, white motion picture screen. There is no picture on the screen because in a moment you will be projecting on this screen an image of the person or persons you want most to forgive.

Now, as the velvet curtains are completely opened and the complete motion picture screen is in view, the theater is darkened, completely. You are completely relaxed in your chair. There now comes into focus on the motion picture screen an image of the person or persons you need to forgive. The image is becoming clearer and clearer. You see this image with all of the details; the hair, eyes, mouth, expressions, and any other details you wish to include. (Pause as the details come into view.)

Now, as you have the picture on the screen in its full intensity, say these words to him or her or them:

"I fully and freely forgive (*name of person or persons*). I release you mentally and spiritually. I completely forgive everything connected with the matter in question. I am free and you are free. It is a marvelous feeling. It is my day of general amnesty. I release anybody and everybody who has ever hurt me mentally or physically, and I wish for each and every one health, happiness, wealth, and all the blessings of life. I do this freely and joyously and from now on, when I think of you, I will say, I have released you and all the blessings of life are yours. I am free and you are free. It is wonderful."

After you have completely forgiven, you may open your eyes and enjoy the feeling of freedom you now have from the negativity of animosity. If this person comes to your mind after this, you have only to say mentally, "Peace be with you."

What if you can't forgive?

Now, if you honestly believe you cannot forgive someone, that the harm and damage done to you was too great, you may do this: when you have completely relaxed in the "motion picture theater" and the image of the person comes to view, you may say, "God, please forgive this person in my name. I cannot do it. I know *you* can forgive him and I will thus be released."

This simple method has seemingly worked miracles in numerous cases. The persons involved have said that for the first time in their lives they have felt complete freedom. They had been locked in the prison of their own minds through feelings of hatred, resentment, and animosity. You and you alone can make the decision to unlock the door and set yourself free.

One woman had thought she could never forgive a person who had physically abused her when she was a child. Her mind was filled with hatred toward him even though she had not seen or heard of him for years. She had allowed herself to get fat, for two reasons: first, because it was subconsciously a protection against such abuse in the future; and, second, the loathing she felt for him had turned toward herself.

It is a little-known fact that your subconscious mind does not distinguish between a negative feeling for another person and one for yourself. In other words, the hatred felt by the student mentioned above for the person who had abused her had been turned around; she hated herself.

When she released the matter to God, and asked that God forgive this person because she could not do it herself, the "miracle" happened. She was completely released and free for the first time in many years. She said she felt like a new person. Of course, her weight problem was corrected within a few months. As soon as the emotional cause is corrected, the physical correction is a simple matter.

Forgiveness unlocks the door

Remember, no matter what the difficulty is, you must unlock the door of your mind through forgiveness. You are the *only* one who can make the decision. By knowing this truth you can be free.

Chapter 9

Mind Barriers

An interesting phenomenon occurs at one point in your subconscious programing. If you are not aware of it, you will be fooled into thinking that something has gone wrong.

With some people this phenomenon occurs within a two- or three-week period. With others it takes longer, but it happens with everyone. Therefore, be alert and aware of it.

The phenomenon is this: you will experience a resistance, a feeling that all is hopeless, that this method won't work any more than any of the others you have tried. Or perhaps you will think how silly this all is, or how useless, etc. When you experience these feelings, be glad because it proves that you are making progress.

Here is the reason for this strange happening in your mind. When you first begin saying your affirmations and using your creative imagination, all seems to go well—for a while. Then, unexpectedly there seems to be a reversal. Things seem to be futile. You may feel you don't even care any more and you may wonder what is happening.

The new confronts the old

You have probably had a negative state of mind for a good many years. When you first start changing your attitude and reprograming your negativity to positiveness, all goes smoothly. Then the new beliefs you have been affirming and the new image you have been projecting meet resistance from the old, solidified, entrenched, false, and limited beliefs. Agitation results and your subconscious mind tries for a short time to convince you it is not worth it; to stay with the old, tried, negative ways. In effect, it is saying to you, "Let's not change things; we don't know what the new ways will be like. We're familiar with the old, tried ways."

If at that point you persist, however, the positive affirmations and imaging will quickly begin to neutralize the negative, limited beliefs.

So, when you begin to feel this resistance, rejoice, because you have hit hard at your old hard-core negative beliefs—negative beliefs that up to this time have led you down a path of depression and anxiety.

Persist and you will succeed

If you do persist, very shortly after this period your subconscious will be completely reprogramed with a new body image and the positive belief that you do like yourself, unconditionally. *Persistence* is the secret to overcoming this mind resistance and barrier.

A few years ago, sleep-teaching was popular and many people bought and tried to use sleep-teaching machines. At that time so little was known about the functioning of the mind that anyone hitting against this mind barrier naturally thought the whole project was foolish and usually gave it up. Now it is known this is a natural occurrence and if a person will just persist the resistance will quickly be overcome.

One student hit this mind barrier even before it had been explained in class. She came one evening and before anyone even had time to say, "Hello," or to make any comment, she burst out with, "I think this whole thing is a lot of silliness. I'm tired of even trying. It won't work any better than anything else I have tried!" The instructor said, "Wonderful! I'm glad to hear you say that. You are really making progress." Both the student and the rest of the class were rather startled to hear that kind of reaction.

The instructor went on to explain how the two levels of mind, the conscious and subconscious, interact. She began by making sure all the students understood that there is only one mind, but that the mind has two very different modes. They interact and work together, but few people understand how this interaction takes place.

We do know that we do not use our full mind capacity. William James, one of America's foremost psychologists, said that no one uses more than 10 percent of his mind's capabilities, for the very simple reason that no one knows how! It has been only within the last few years that much knowledge has been obtained concerning how the mind functions and how interactions between conscious and subconscious are accomplished. There is still a great deal to be discovered about this "world within" all of us. We know more about the moon than we know about our own minds.

You really can reprogram your own mind

The little we do know has been discovered only within the last few years. Much of this discovery interestingly coincides with the development of computers. The story goes that two computer scientists were speculating during their lunch hour as to whether the human mind works on the same general principle as their computers. They did some experimentation and noted that the human mind can indeed be programed—in much the same way as computers are programed.

That is the principle, a "law" of the subconscious mind—that it is "programed." This does not mean that you are a machine; it merely means you have a "machine" to direct and use. The conscious part of your mind can make the decisions and do the programing and the subconscious part carries out the programed instructions.

Computers are programed by computer programers, writing a step-by-step program the computers are to execute. Computers rarely make mistakes; but programers often do. When they do make a mistake, or when the material inserted into the computer is trivial or wrong, the expression is, "GIGO—garbage in, garbage out." And so it is with the human mind. There is a great deal of "garbage" in our mind's programing; and, as in computer language, "garbage in, garbage out."

For example, several hundred years ago, most people believed the earth was flat. Any decision made regarding travel on the high seas required the so-called "fact" of the earth's being flat to be taken into consideration. "Should we make that distant journey and risk falling off the edge of the earth?" men may have asked themselves. Of course, we now know that this basic "fact" was nothing but "garbage," but at that time it was known as a "truth." So it is with our minds today. We have programed in our subconscious mind many negatives that we think are "truths," when in reality they are nothing but "garbage."

As has been discussed, many of these negatives were programed into our minds at an early age, so we had no defense against them. But now we know the truth, and we can do something about the "garbage" that needs to be discarded.

The conscious mind is the deciding, reasoning, and judging factor of the mind. The subconscious mind not only controls the involuntary functions of your body such as breathing, heartbeat, digestive system, etc., but also obeys your conscious orders. All of your habit patterns, both good and bad, are located in your subconscious mind—as are memory files and other possible functions such as extrasensory perception (ESP).

Your conscious mind directs

Your conscious mind decides, for example, that you will walk over to the bookshelf and get a certain book. In deciding to do that, the conscious mind alerts the subconscious mind and it moves the muscles in your legs to walk you over to the bookshelf and moves the muscles in your arm to pick up the book, and it will direct your eyes to read the titles, etc. A simplified outline indeed, but remember that your conscious mind is the directing factor. Your subconscious mind only obeys the dictates of the conscious mind—both good and bad directives. It really doesn't care; it only obeys.

Because all of your habit patterns are programed into your subconscious mind, you sometimes do things you do not want to do—such as eating a strawberry sundae while on a strict 500-calorie diet. This is an automatic, involuntary response based on the programing in your subconscious mind. This is an example of the only circumstances in which your subconscious mind will not obey the dictates of your conscious mind. When your will power comes into conflict with your subconscious programing, the programing will always win. This is why it is so important to change the negative programing.

We know that the emotions have a great deal of influence in our weight problems. If we feel alone or unloved, eating helps to fill the void. So it is that in the course of a diet—and going great—we experience an incident that makes us feel unloved. Then we have that sundae—even though consciously we had decided to stay on our 500-calorie diet!

The subconscious versus will power

Your subconscious programing is more powerful than your will power in any situation where the two are in direct conflict. This is why you must change your programing before you can make any permanent changes in your weight.

When the student, mentioned earlier, hit the mind barrier and became so upset, this is the very thing that had happened to her. Her will power had come into conflict with her subconscious programing and a great deal of agitation had resulted. She had encountered the programing that previously had led her to underestimate her real self-worth. In attempting to say the master affirmation, "I like myself unconditionally," for 21 days, she had hit her previous negative programing and its force and resistance were surprising to her. This encounter was then interpreted to her conscious mind as, "It's no use, it won't work, it's just silly, etc." If you do not have such resistance, then you like yourself very much indeed. In that case, your battle may be much easier. However, that is the exception rather than the rule.

There is indeed much more to the inner working of the mind than you had probably imagined. In fact, science has barely begun to understand what your "billion-dollar computer," your mind, can really do.

Chapter 10

You Have the Keys; Unlock the Prison

As you can see, the plan of mental dieting is a method of reprograming your subconscious "computer" for awareness—awareness of the best way of eating, of the underlying psychological reasons for food "binges." You now know that, if properly programed, your subconscious mind can and will take over and correct your weight problem.

Your subconscious mind "knows" your particular body chemistry much better than anyone else, including weight-loss clinic leaders, doctors, or friends—or even yourself. It can reveal to you your proper weight for your body and keep it at that weight for the rest of your life without your ever doing anything consciously about it—but only *if* your mind is properly programed.

121

We have just now begun to realize, through research on obesity, that there is much more to losing weight than merely going on a 500- or 1000-calorie diet. There is even more to keeping the weight off once it has been lost. Millions of people have gone on every kind of a diet imaginable, and lost weight—only to gain it back as soon as they have gone off the diet. Only a very small percentage lose weight and keep it lost.

Knowledge is power

You may think that some of the many topics covered in the mental dieting plan are not related, yet they are because all of these procedures will reprogram your "billion-dollar computer"—your mind—with the correct information and data. This correct information will erase the "garbage" that may now plague your mind.

Goal-setting, diet information, calorie information, exercise programing, all contribute correct data to your "computer." This includes knowledge of all of the psychological reasons why you go on food "binges." Data concerning your body's appestat and how it can be set—all of these things are very important input for your subconscious mind programing. Self-image psychology and how it relates to your weight problem is an important concept for you to understand.

All of these things are discussed for only one reason: to help you reprogram your own subconscious "computer" to take over the natural process of selecting the proper food for your special body chemistry. Your mind should take over this process as it now controls all your involuntary functions, such as heartbeat, breathing, or digestion. It does a splendid job with all of those functions. Now let it also include the ideal weight and body image for you. Once programed with correct information, it can and will do a far better job than you have been able to do up to this time.

New freedom from "dieting"

When your programing is completed you will have attained your ideal body image and you will be able to have it as long as you live without having to use will power every time you go to a party or restaurant where all of your favorite foods are being served. When your "billion-dollar computer" is properly programed, you can eat and enjoy good food and drink to a degree you never before have experienced because you know that the next day or perhaps for several days after the party, you will have a diminished appetite as your "computer" gets you back on the beam. You know this to be true if you have ever successfully used the mental exercises to program yourself against sweets and carbohydrates, and have found you had no appetite for these foods.

So, in effect, your subconscious mind has now taken control of your appestat; it has said to you, "All right, you've had your fun, now I'll control your appetite until those calories are worked out of your system." The beautiful part of this is that absolutely no effort or will power is required. You are simply not so hungry for several days.

The muscle tone exercises, using your towel and jump rope (Chapter 3), are all the exercise you need for superb muscle tone. Of course, this also includes the abdominal exercise to firm your stomach muscles. The results you get from the few seconds per day you spend on these exercises is certainly worth the small effort required.

The flash-cue method, the "cue cards" (Chapter 5) will help flash instructions to your subconscious "computer" in times of emergency. You may also use this method when you need to resist a particular temptation. Your cue cards will help you to desire a wholesome, nutritious meal instead of coffee and doughnuts.

Remember to use the "words of power," or affirmations which also cue your mind into the reprograming process quickly (Chapter 5).

The vitamin-mineral supplements mentioned earlier (Chapter 3) are necessary to supplement the diet while you are in the process of the reprograming so you will not have "hidden hunger." And they will become attractive to you in your ongoing nutritional choices.

All of these things are for only one purpose: to

provide data for your "billion-dollar computer" so
that it may assume subconscious control, so that will
power will no longer be necessary to obtain and
maintain your ideal body image.

A powerful new self-image

To repeat, the most important part of mental dieting is your own subconscious programing to aid your
creative imagination (the mind's power factor) in
changing the "fat image" you now have in your mind
into a "slim image."

This is accomplished by generating a "feeling"—a
feeling of liking yourself, of believing in yourself—a
feeling of "knowingness" inside of you that tells you
that you are worthy of an ideal body image. You will
be creating an experience for your subconscious mind
so that a pattern will be "etched" into your brain
cells—a pattern that your mind will follow, a "slim"
pattern instead of a "fat" pattern.

You were born to have a good self-image, the
realization of the potential you had as a baby, a
potential that may as yet be unrealized through no
fault of your own. The imprint of a good self-image
is still there, but it has superimposed on it a false
image of unworthiness through negative programing
in your early years.

By using the simple tools you have just read
about, you will generate a feeling of joy within
yourself that tells you that you are a worthy human

being. Once you have that feeling, you will know that you have changed the untrue or false "fat" image to the true "slim" image.

This concept is so new that it is necessary to know why you are doing the various things explained in this book. You must have a background for the concept in order to be motivated to follow the procedures outlined in the next chapter.

You now realize why the psychological steps described must be taken in their exact sequence in order for the reprograming to work.

This book shows you the way; now the action is up to you!

You have the key to open the prison of your mind, so that you, too, can be free.

Chapter 11

More 'Slim' Tips

In Chapter 1 you were told that you are a prisoner of your own mind; that you, and you alone, have kept yourself locked tightly within the confines of your own thinking. As you now know, much erroneous thinking was programed into your subconscious mind in early childhood. You have, up to this time, accepted this negative thinking as a "truth." You cannot "blame" anyone for this restricted thinking because until a few short years ago no one knew very much about how the human mind works.

However, now you have some knowledge about this; and, if you now do nothing to unlock the door of your "mind-prison" you have only yourself to blame!

A proven method

This book is an "awareness" book, a book written to make you aware of your own marvelous potential, your creativity, the tremendous power of your own mind. The information presented here is backed by the actual experiences of many people, over a period of eight years; people who have proven to themselves and to their families and friends that the moment they become aware of and accept their own latent creative mind energy, *the "world is theirs."*

You have noted by now that the methods in this book can be used in many areas of your life: in business and family relationships, and in friendship relations. They are not restricted to the problems of weight control.

To become aware of something is *always* the key to being able to do something about it or to utilize it. So it is with your mind; once you become aware of how your conscious and subconscious interact, you are in control, and can decide exactly what you want to do.

Some helpful specifics

This chapter contains several additional, specific mental exercises. The first one is designed to program your subconscious mind against sweets of all kinds. The next is to program your subconscious mind against starches, or empty carbohydrates. There is also a mental exercise to allow your subconscious to tell you what your ideal weight should be. Even though you may consciously have set a weight goal, that goal could well be the result of erroneous "programing." Your subconscious mind "knows" what your ideal weight should be, much better than any weight chart, doctor, or even weight clinic.

Also presented in this chapter is a diet to be used during the 21-day programing period outlined in earlier chapters. It is advisable to stay on this diet so that you can get a head start toward your weight-loss objectives while you are reprograming your subconscious mind. It is a high-protein, low-carbohydrate, low-calorie diet. When your programing is completed, you do not have to stay on any diet. However, until that time, it will be helpful to follow the diet suggested in this chapter.

There are also tips on "slim" cooking. After you complete your mental programing, you will not want heavy, weight-producing foods. You will desire only "slim" foods, so some tips on preparing them are presented here.

Also provided is a daily maintenance calorie chart that tells you what you should consume each day in order to maintain your "ideal body image." After this information is programed into your mind, you will not find it necessary to refer to this chart. Until then it will help you to do so.

Through research we know that your body responds best to alternating periods of rest and exercise, so the best informationn on this method is also included. There are also more "words of power," or affirmations, that will be helpful in your programing.

"Theories are fine but action always does the work."

The "tools" in this chapter

In summary, here are the specific helps that follow in this order:

1. Alpha awareness exercise for *programing against sweets.*

2. Alpha awareness exercise for *programing against starches and carbohydrates.*

3. Alpha awareness exercise for *discerning the "ideal weight"* for your particular body structure.

4. "Slim" *cooking.*

5. Four major pointers to get more nourishment from less food.

6. Daily Maintainance *Calorie Chart* and *formula.*

7. Additional *affirmations.*

8. *A diet* for the 21-day mental diet program.

9. *Mental diet alternating exercise and rest program.*

1. *Mental exercise for programing against sweets*
   (Read through the entire exercise before begin-ning.)

You may begin this exercise by holding in your hand two pieces of your favorite candy or sweet, whatever it may be. You are seated in your favorite chair with your feet flat on the floor. You will take three deep breaths, deep to the bottom of your lungs, to rid your system of excess carbon dioxide.

Now take one piece of candy, or whatever you are holding, and smell it—be aware of the odor. Now, while you are at the outer-conscious level of your mind, taste it with the tip of your tongue. Put it in your mouth and savor the flavor, tasting with all of your taste buds. You have "taste sensors" over your entire mouth; notice where they are—on your tongue, the sides of your mouth, in the back of your mouth. On this conscious level, be totally aware of the taste sensation. Now hold your nose and notice what hap-pens to the flavor. Does your sense of smell have anything to do with your tasting the sweets?

You will later do the same taste test when you are at the alpha (or subconscious) level of your mind. Then you will notice an extreme sweetness. But now, hold your nose for a while to see what happens to the flavor of your candy when you no longer smell the odor. Notice what tastes have disappeared. Notice what tastes remain. Later, while at the alpha level you will program yourself against all sweets, but especial-ly against your favorite sweet by using mental imagery in order to be extremely aware of the sweetness in all foods. While at the alpha level, your taste buds are much more sensitive and thus convey a message to your appestat that sweets are *distastefully* sweet.

You may use this same method if you have a problem in using too much sugar in various foods —coffee, for example. Go to the alpha level of consciousness (as described in earlier chapters—and later in this one). Prepare a cup of coffee (or other drink if you don't use coffee) with a fourth of the sugar you usually use. At the alpha level, sip the drink, becoming totally aware of the sweetness. From then on, you will find that this small amount of sugar is all you will desire. Becoming aware of the extreme sweetness of any food will diminish your desire for that sweetness in food in the future.

I knew a woman who used this method on chocolate candy. This had been her temptation almost to the point of obsession. At the alpha level of consciousness she tasted her favorite sweet chocolate candy bar. She said that at once she was totally aware of the extreme sweetness of the candy. It was distastefully sweet. But the "clincher" was when she held her nose while eating her candy at the alpha level. This was a total turnoff because, she said, without the fragrance of the candy, it tasted exactly like wax—tasteless wax. It even had the consistency of wax. From that moment on, her obsession was gone.

Now let us continue the mental exercise for programing against sweets:

You are seated in your favorite chair with your feet flat on the floor. You have in your hand two pieces of your favorite candy. As suggested earlier, begin by eating the first piece and being totally aware of the taste sensations.

Close your eyes, take three deep breaths and, while exhaling, mentally repeat the word *relax* several times, to yourself.

To enter a deeper level of alpha consciousness, take another deep breath and mentally repeat the word *within* several times.

To enter a still deeper level of alpha consciousness, take another deep breath and mentally repeat the words *relax within* several times.

To enable you to enter a deeper, more extended level of alpha consciousness, you will relax all areas of your body beginning at your head and scalp.

As you relax down through each area, you will reach a deeper, more extended level of alpha consciousness and slow your brain's electrical wave pattern to about eight cycles per second. Using your creative imagination, "see" the "wheels" at first revolving very fast and gradually slowing down as you are relaxing from the top of your head down to the very tips of your toes. As the wheels revolve more and more slowly, you are feeling more and more peaceful and relaxed.

With your creative imagination, imagine relaxing your scalp and the top of your head. Imagine relaxing your forehead and face muscles. Allow your teeth to separate slightly. Allow this sensation of relaxation to flow slowly downward throughout the entire body all the way down to your toes.

Now, imagine relaxing your neck and shoulders, relax the arms and hands and imagine this relaxation slowly flowing downward—and the wheels are slowing down; now are turning very slowly.

Now, imagine relaxing your back muscles, your chest muscles and your abdominal muscles, imagine this relaxation flowing downward—all the way down to your toes.

It's such a pleasant feeling to be so deeply relaxed.

You are now in a deeper, more extended level of alpha consciousness and the wheels are turning very, very slowly now.

To enter an even deeper, more extended level, imagine yourself in a serene, relaxing setting; your perfect place of relaxation, wherever that may be. Spend about five minutes at your ideal place and allow yourself to relax even more completely. Take a deep breath and enter an even deeper level, with the wheels revolving ever so slowly.

Now, if you feel yourself to be at the alpha level—you can tell by recognizing your personal "benchmarks"—you will be totally aware of the taste sensation of the piece of candy. Remember, your "benchmark" is your own particular sensation, or seeing colors, or feeling a light feeling—the "signal" you recognize every time you get to the alpha level. It always happens at that level.

As soon as you get to the alpha level, put the other piece of candy into your mouth and once again savor the flavor, tasting with all of your taste sensors. Be totally aware of the taste sensation over your entire mouth. Notice the extreme sweetness, the distastefully sweet flavor; it actually is sickeningly sweet. Now hold your nose and be aware of what happens to the taste. Has the flavor of the candy disappeared? Is there just a gritty sensation left, or a waxy feeling in your mouth? Or perhaps it tastes like a piece of cardboard.

Now, use your creative imagination to program yourself against all sweets in the future. See yourself being aware of the distastefully sweet sensation and see yourself saying *no* and having absolutely no desire to even taste it. Spend a few minutes visualizing and experiencing this in much detail, both the picturing and the tasting. Say the master affirmation to yourself three times: *I like myself unconditionally*.

Now, slowly stretch your arms over your head, flex your muscles and come out of the alpha level of your mind and into the beta (or fully conscious) level. You have now "reprogramed" against sweets. You will be able to tell if your programing has been completed by your reaction to sweets in the future.

Repeat this exercise as many times as necessary to completely erase all cravings.

2. *Mental exercise for programing against carbohydrates*

(Read entire exercise before beginning.)

You may begin this exercise by holding in your hand two crackers (or potato chips or french fries—whatever your extreme temptation in the carbohydrate food group happens to be). Take the cracker, or whatevever you have, and smell it, being aware of the odor. Now taste it with the tip of your tongue—while you are still at the conscious level of your mind, the beta level. Now put it into your mouth and savor the flavor, tasting with all of your tasting ability. Use the tastebuds on your tongue, the sensors of the sides of your mouth, and in the back of your mouth. Be totally aware of the taste sensation—on the conscious level. Now hold your nose and notice what happens to the flavor.

Now, let's go down to the alpha level of your mind and repeat these procedures.

You are seated comfortably in your favorite chair with your feet flat on the floor. Close your eyes, take three deep breaths; and, while exhaling, mentally repeat the word *relax* several times to yourself.

To enter a deeper level of alpha awareness, take another deep breath and mentally repeat the word *within* several times.

To enter a still deeper level of alpha awareness, take another deep breath and mentally repeat the words *relax within* several times.

To enable yourself to enter an even deeper, more extended level of alpha consciousness, you will relax all areas of your body beginning at your head and scalp.

As you relax down through each area, you will reach a deeper, more extended level of alpha consciousness and slow your brain wave pattern to about eight cycles per second. Using your creative imagination, "see" the "wheels" revolving very fast and then gradually slowing down as you are relaxing, from the top of your head down to the very tips of your toes. As the wheels revolve more and more slowly, you are feeling more and more peaceful and relaxed.

With your creative imagination, imagine relaxing your scalp and the top of your head. Imagine relaxing your forehead and face muscles. Allow your teeth to separate slightly. Allow this sensation of relaxation to flow slowly downward throughout the entire body—all the way down to your toes.

Now, imagine relaxing your neck and shoulders, relax the arms and hands, and imagine this relaxation slowly flowing downward. The wheels are beginning to slow down and now are turning very slowly.

Now, imagine relaxing your back muscles, your chest muscles, and your abdominal muscles. Imagine this relaxation flowing downward—all the way down to the toes.

Now, imagine relaxing down through your hips and legs, through the calves and feet—all the way down to the toes.

It's such a pleasant feeling to be so deeply relaxed.

You are now in a deeper, more extended level of alpha consciousness and the wheels are now turning very, very slowly.

To enter an even deeper, more extended level, imagine yourself in a serene, relaxing setting, your perfect place of relaxation, wherever that may be. Spend about five minutes at your ideal place of relax-

ation, and allow yourself to relax even more completely. Take a deep breath and enter an even deeper
level with the wheels revolving ever so slowly. Now
make sure you are at the alpha level by recognizing
your personal "benchmarks" (as have been previously
described).

If you are at a good, deep level, proceed with the
taste test.

Put the cracker, or potato chip, on the tip of your
tongue and taste it. Taste it with your entire tasting
"equipment"—your tongue, the sides of your mouth,
the roof of your mouth—being totally aware of the
taste of the food. Be aware of as many flavors as you
can distinguish. Now take a bite and listen to the
crunching sound it makes. Smell the cracker and see
if smelling it makes the flavor more distinct.

Now, while you are down at the alpha level,
remember that your cracker, or potato chip, or french
fry, or whatever you have, is made up of empty
calories that will give you only inadequate nourishment. Empty carbohydrates from now on will have a
pasty, dull flavor for you and you will not enjoy them
anymore. Program yourself to notice the pasty, dull
flavor and see how much it resembles a piece of
cardboard, especially when you hold your nose and
the odor sense is gone. Empty carbohydrates include
all foods such as potato chips, white bread, pastries,
and all other starchy foods.

Now program yourself by using your creative
imagination and seeing yourself sitting down at a
dinner table, and saying *no* to any and every empty

carbohydrate food, being acutely aware of the fact
that even if you did eat it, it would have nothing but
a dull, pasty flavor like a piece of cardboard.

Now, while still down at the alpha level, program
yourself to realize that protein foods, such as eggs,
cheese, and meat, will set your appestat at an even
level and keep you from getting hungry. See yourself
really enjoying them; realizing that they will quickly
turn to energy—so you have an added bonus. These
foods will make you into a dynamic person, full of
vitality and energy, enjoying life to the fullest.

Also see yourself sitting at your table, enjoying a
green salad. The salad has crisp, green lettuce;
crunchy pieces of celery; cool, pale, sliced cucumbers;
small bright-red salad tomatoes; and any other raw
vegetables you really enjoy. Add to your imaginary
salad anything else you like such as smooth, green,
sliced avocadoes; crisp, red radishes; slivers of bright
orange carrots, etc. Put on this delightful salad the
dressing of your choice, and top it with all the "trim-
mings," diced cheese, sliced eggs or whatever you
like.

As you eat this salad, you can "feel" each
mouthful of it turn into vitality and energy in your
body. This kind of fuel in your body imparts the ra-
diance of health to every cell of your body. Visualize
this for a few moments, and try to experience all the
various taste sensations. Before coming out of the
alpha level, say the master affirmation to yourself
three times: *I like myself unconditionally.*

Now, slowly stretch your arms over your head,

flex your muscles, and come out of the alpha level of your mind and into the beta level, the conscious level. Now you have programed yourself *against* empty carbohydrates, and *for* protein and green salads.

3. *Mental exercise for allowing your subconscious mind to tell you what your ideal weight should be for your particular body structure.*

Using the standard method of relaxation and going to the alpha level of your mind will allow your subconscious to perceive what your ideal body weight should be. Your subconscious mind "knows" you better than do your doctor, your friends—or even yourself at the conscious level. If you will allow it to "talk" to you, you will get much help and information about yourself. However, there is no way of getting in touch with it except through the method of relaxation and going to the alpha, or subconscious level.

Again, as previously described, begin by sitting in your favorite chair, with your feet flat on the floor, with your hands loosely in your lap. Close your eyes, take three deep breaths. While exhaling, mentally repeat the word *relax* several times to yourself.

To enter a deeper level of alpha consciousness, take another deep breath and mentally repeat the word *within*, several times.

To enter a still deeper level of alpha consciousness, take another deep breath and mentally repeat the words *relax within* several times.

To enable you to enter an even deeper, more extended level of alpha consciousness, you will relax all areas of your body beginning at your head and scalp.

As you relax down through each area, you will reach a deeper, more extended level of alpha consciousness and you will slow your brain wave pattern to about eight cycles per second. Using your creative imagination, "see" the "wheels" revolving very fast and then gradually slowing down as you are relaxing, from the top of your head down to the very tips of your toes. As the wheels revolve more and more slowly, you are feeling more and more peacefully relaxed.

With your creative imagination, imagine relaxing your scalp and the top of your head. Imagine relaxing your forehead and face muscles. Allow your teeth to separate slightly. Allow this sensation of relaxation to flow slowly downward through the entire body—all the way down to your toes.

Now, imagine relaxing your neck and shoulders, relax your arms and hands, and imagine this relaxation slowly flowly downward; the wheels are beginning to slow down and now are turning very slowly.

Now, imagine relaxing your back muscles, your chest muscles, and your abdominal muscles. Imagine this relaxation flowing downward, all the way down to the toes.

Now, imagine relaxing your hips and legs, down through the calves and feet—all the way down to the toes.

It's such a pleasant feeling to be so deeply relaxed. You are now in a deeper, more extended level of alpha consciousness and the wheels are now turning very, very slowly.

To enter an even deeper, more extended level, imagine yourself in your peaceful, relaxing setting. Spend a few minutes there. Now, you are at a deep level of alpha consciousness.

Using your creative imagination, see before you, in your mind's eye, a large, old-fashioned scale. See the numerals on the face of the scale. Right now, the pointer is at zero. Step forward and up on the platform of this large, old-fashioned scale. See yourself standing on the scale now, and the pointer starts slowly to move upward from zero. You watch it intensely; slowly it moves up and up. It stops at a numeral, hovers for a moment, and moves up a little and then down a little, and finally after a slight quiver, stops at your ideal weight! It may, or it may not, be the same weight goal you have adopted. However, your subconscious "knows" better than anyone else what your ideal weight should be.

4. *"Slim" cooking*

What is "slim" cooking? It means the kind of cooking you will enjoy for the rest of your life. It means using wholesome, natural, lean foods. It means no overcooking. Cooking your foods only as long as necessary for maximum goodness—and no more—means that you will receive more nutrition. In the case of most vegetables, this means only a few minutes. It means being stingy in the use of fats, sugars, and thickeners; wasting no money on pastries and rich sauces or cakes. Instead, use your money for lean meats, lean fish, poultry, (or good meat substitutes if you are a vegetarian), "lean" milk, fresh fruits, and vegetables. Make your foods tastier by using herbs, vegetable salts, and spices. If you use a sweetener at all, use honey or molasses.

If you use meat, remember that the most expensive cuts are not necessary in order to have lean meat. In fact, the cheaper cuts contain more nourishment than the most expensive cuts. It is a simple matter to tenderize them. Trim off all visible fat. Cook the meat correctly—that means broiling or roasting. If you are roasting meats, do it in a slow oven.

Have some protein for breakfast, because this keeps your blood sugar level on an even keel and "sets" your appestat.

5. *Four major pointers to get more nourishment from less food*

a. Eat slowly in a relaxed, peaceful atmosphere.

b. Include complete proteins with each meal.

c. Cut carbohydrates (starches and sugar) to a minimum (you must have some, such as those in whole wheat bread).

d. Chew your food twice as long. You will have twice the pleasure, it will help your blood sugar level to rise, and you will feel nourished and satisfied with less food. In this way, you will experience real pleasure in eating less!

6. *Daily maintenance calories**

To maintain your weight, you should eat only the following calories per day, after you are at your ideal body weight.

Women

Weight	25 yrs.	45 yrs.	65 yrs.
99	1,900	1,800	1,500
110	2,050	1,950	1,600
121	2,200	2,050	1,750
128	2,300	2,200	1,800
132	2,300	2,200	1,850
143	2,500	2,300	2,000
154	2,600	2,450	2,050
165	2,750	2,600	2,150

Men

Weight	25 yrs.	45 yrs.	65 yrs.
110	2,500	2,350	1,950
121	2,700	2,550	2,150
132	2,850	2,700	2,250
143	3,000	2,800	2,350
154	3,200	3,000	2,550
165	3,400	3,200	2,700
176	3,500	3,350	2,800
187	3,700	3,500	2,900

* Based on moderate activity. If your life is very physically active, add calories; if you lead a sedentary life, subtract calories.

You can see what you are doing by assimilating all this calorie information, learning about the appestat and the psychological reasons for overeating. You are "programing your computer," your subconscious mind, for awareness. Unless you do that, your subconscious mind has no information on which to act.

Formula for reaching your goal weight. (An example.)

143 pounds (what you weigh now)
−128 pounds (what you want to weigh)
15 pounds overweight

Multiply the 15 pounds of excess weight by 3,500: 15 x 3,500 = 52,500, or the number of calories you must cut in order to achieve 128 pounds. (One pound of excess fat contains 3,500 calories.)

7. *Some additional mental diet affirmations*

"I now like and concentrate on eating only good, nutritional, low-calorie foods."

"It is pleasant and easy for me to lose weight."

"I am succeeding in losing weight, with confidence, courage, faith, and sincerity."

"I always have good, positive thoughts about myself."

"When I achieve my ideal body image, I will be able to retain it with ease."

"I say my affirmations at least twice a day, and oftener if possible."

"I go to the alpha level, my subconscious mind, at

least twice a day and use my creative imagination to picture my ideal body image."

"I use the flash cue method (Chapter 5) to resist temptations whenever I need to."

Remember the master affirmation, "*I Like Myself Unconditionally!*"

Say the above affirmation the first thing upon arising in the morning and the last thing before going to bed at night. Use a mental picture each time and hold this mental image in your mind for six seconds.

8. *A diet for the 21-day mental diet program*

During your 21-day "reprograming" period it is advisable to use the following diet. When your subconscious programing is completed you will no longer need this or any other planned diet.

Daily protein

4 ounces of lean meat, fish, or fowl daily. Can be: chicken breast (skin removed), calf liver, lean veal, fish.

A meat substitute or protein supplement such as "Superpro" may be used instead of meat. The supplement can be dissolved in unsweetened grapefruit juice or tomato juice (no orange juice).

Daily vegetables

Choose two servings daily from the following (½ to ¾ cup):

Asparagus	Celery	Lettuce	Summer squash
Salad greens	Spinach	Tomatoes	Watercress
Beet greens	Chard	Onions	Mushrooms
Bean sprouts	Fennel	Chicory	Cucumbers
Cabbage	Kale	Radishes	String beans

Daily fruit

Choose only one fruit daily:

½ Grapefruit
1 Apple
1 Orange
1 Handful of fresh strawberries

Seasonings

Any kind of herb seasoning, dried or fresh.
Juice of one lemon or lime daily.
Vinegar-and-oil dressing.
Salt in moderation.
Artificial sweeteners (no sugar)—if you don't object to the chemical aspects.

Bread

Choose one of the following daily:

1 bread stick
1 piece melba toast
½ slice rye bread
¼ cup wheat germ

Beverages

Fresca or sugar-free Shasta (you may not favor the chemicals)
Coffee (no sugar, but may use Coffee-mate)
Sanka
Tea
Consommé or bouillon
Lots of water (at least 6 to 8 glasses daily). This is a must.

Special supplements

Lecithin—2 tsps. daily (or capsule)
Calcium tablets
Vitamin E and vitamin C
All-purpose vitamin and mineral capsule

9. *Mental diet alternating exercise and rest program*

The latest research has shown that the body needs a balanced program of both rest and exercise. Follow this program for the three weeks of your reprograming period—if there are no health problems that should restrict your exercise.

1. Each morning when you awaken, stretch all of your muscles. (You may use the towel exercise [Chapter 3].)

2. Monday, Wednesday and Friday: jump rope for a count of 200 jumps. (Work up to it gradually: begin with 50 on Monday, 100 Wednesday, 200 on Friday.)

3. Tuesday, Thursday, and Saturday: do your favorite exercise such as tennis, swimming, bicycle riding, bowling, etc.

4. Wednesday: go to bed early!

5. On either Saturday or Sunday: take a nap!

After the three-week programing period is over, do the above for three weeks in every month. On the fourth week of every month, don't do any special exercise; just rest.

After your subconscious programing is completed, you may eat and exercise as your programing prompts you. Until that time, you should stay with this diet and exercise program.

Master affirmations

"These affirmations will reprogram my subconscious mind and dissolve all the mental blocks that have kept me from obtaining my weight-loss goal."

Each morning, the first thing upon arising, look

into your mirror, deep into your eyes, and say aloud: *I like myself unconditionally!*

Each evening, the last thing before retiring, look into the mirror, deep into your eyes, and again say aloud: *I like myself unconditionally!*

As many times during the day as you remember, say this to yourself. Or write this affirmation on a small card and read it to yourself. Do this for 21 days in succession and you will be amazed at the results.

Use this "feedback" affirmation: "Every day, twice or more, I will say the above affirmation."

————•·•————

Now you know one of the great secrets of the universe—that the world reflects, as a giant mirror, exactly what your self-image is. As you raise your self-image and realize that you are deserving of a beautiful appearance, *this* image is reflected back to you with the message: "You are a wonderful human being!"

Personal notes and observations

Use the following pages for making further notations about your goals and progress as well as your own special discoveries in this new adventure in creative awareness. Please share your experiences with us, if you wish, by writing to the author. See the very last page for information about additional helps available.

Cassette tapes available

The following cassette tapes are available to help you reprogram your mind for a "slim" image and teach you how to relax. It has been found in our classes that "learning time" has been cut in half by use of the tapes.

Tape No. 1

Side 1: *World Within* (basics of relaxation).

Side 2: *Ideal Body Image* (learning to use your creative imagination to visualize your ideal body).

Tape No. 2

Side 1: *Progressive Relaxation* (to make a "brain cell impression" for relaxation).

Side 2: *Tunnel Relaxation* (helps to "float" to your conscious mind early childhood food experiences that were programed into your mind).

Tape No. 3

Side 1: *Sound of the Bells* (learning how to relax with background of five bells, the bells affecting the subconscious in totally unexpected ways–based on an oriental theory of musical harmonics that makes relaxation a total experience).

Side 2: *Sound of the Bells* (helping you to visualize your ideal body image).

Tape No. 4

Side 1: *Imprinting "Brain Cell Impressions" for Relaxation* (learning the difference between tension and relaxation.

Side 2: *Heartbeat* (the heartbeat rhythm being tuned to universal subconscious and autonomic responses to enable you to both relax and visualize your ideal body).

The above cassette tapes are exclusively for helping you to "learn relaxation" and to achieve your ideal body image.

The tapes are not produced or sold by the publisher of this book and are listed here only as a matter of possible interest to the reader.

They may be ordered directly from: Seminars of Self-Awareness, Box 202, Pinedale, California 93650, at $10 for each tape, plus 50 cents postage and handling.

Other tapes are available to help achieve other goals such as stopping the smoking habit, learning how to use your creative imagination, tapping into your subconscious mind's creativity, learning to know yourself, and more.

For a listing of these other subjects, send a card with your address to the above address.